AROUND THE WORLD IN 51 AND 1/2 DAYS

"The Victorian era spawned a whole generation of fainting, restless women who overcame their delicate colonial constitutions to travel the world in stiff bonnets and inconvenient corsetry. So our plan to make a romantically tortuous voyage from Japan to London largely overland was far from unique. However, we like to think that we did it with less grace, more sincerity, and infinitely less cumbersome underwear than the average Victorian heroine. In graphic detail this tale relates anecdotes of bureaucracy, banditry, gastronomic peril, near-abductions averted only by the timely blow of a lucky whistle and uncomfortably close encounters with wildlife and other travellers...all with refreshing disregard for our own street credibility or hopes of being granted a visa for a return visit anytime soon. Japan, Hong Kong, China, Outer Mongolia. Siberia, Moscow, all in 51 and a half days; a journey full of learning, cliched reflection and utter, utter exhilaration--bordering on hysteria at times, as we grapple with the bewildering challenges each day's travel brings..."

ISBN: 1-928781-06-3

Published by Hollis Books

Artwork and Photos by Kirsti Shields
All rights reserved

Cover by Hollis Books

AROUND THE WORLD
IN 51 AND 1/2
DAYS

KIRSTI SHIELDS

HOLLIS BOOKS

AROUND THE WORLD IN 51 AND A HALF DAYS

PROLOGUE

The unofficial travellers creed is quite specific about the distinction between tourist and traveller. Any self-respecting "traveller" must expect to run a vicious gauntlet of gastronomic gaffs and endless, endless toileting tragedies; to provide general merriment to local people by confusing commonplace household nouns with the words for amusing body parts; and to dip at least a few times a week to a state of imminent medical crisis. In summary , to prostrate oneself at the altar of certain humiliation at least seventeen times a day.

We had been living in Japan for a year by the time the idea for this trip was conceived, and felt we could open a small consultancy firm offering corporate seminars on any of the above. What we hadn't taken into account was the unique scope for blunder that each country was able to offer to the uninitiated traveller. From muggings in Mongolia and bandits in Siberia to spiders in the Gobi desert. Not to mention bicycles and bureaucracy and bullies in Beijing and a whole pot of life-endangering dining experiences regrettably containing the word gizzard.

It was ironic that the idea for this trip had, for me, been conceived from the seeds of a shaky kind of panic about flying straight back to England from Japan and suddenly finding myself back in the heaving throng of Heathrow Airport with my head lagging eighteen hours behind. This trip, I optimistically anticipated, would be gently reflective and offer all kinds of opportunity to catch up with myself on route. Once the idea that my good friend Laura and I might actually be thinking about tackling such a gargantuan trip, the scathing comments started. A Nordic horseman called Thor told me I wouldn't last a minute in a place without hot running water. The gauntlet was thrown down.

We received a lot of good, and a lot of bad advice before we went. A gentleman in my office cautioned me that the Chinese people he knew would eat anything with four legs except the kitchen table.

Someone else, it could have been my father, cautioned that, despite the best evidence of the world's leading cartographers, Outer Mongolia didn't really exist. It was apparently a diplomatic Bermuda Triangle secretly supplying the White Slave Trade. (This was later corroborated by a Japanese Geography Teacher at one of my village schools.) So, with a certain amount of trepidation, a few hazy but unreliable preconceptions and lots and lots of writing paper, we embarked, in the middle of July, the trip that would take us half-way Around the World in Fifty-One and a Half Days.

OUR FIRST NIGHT IN HONG KONG:
WHAT ARE WE DOING HERE?

The need for air never seemed greater than that first night in our windowless Hong-Kong hotel room. Walls the colour of chocolate pudding crept towards us from all sides as we battled the encroaching wave of claustrophobia. The seven keys our landlady had given us raised phantom hopes of hidden windows lurking beneath eight generations of woodchip wall-paper. We scrutinised the minimalistic fittings and fixtures for signs of air-gaps. Laura spotted a faint nub over the doorway and with disproportionate excitement fetched a long stick. Like any graduate of the 1980s with their endless, appalling Indiana Jones movies, we lived in hope of finding a secret door at least once in our lives. The nub proved to be ominously hand-shaped and we wondered with a shiver if the last decorator met a grisly end beneath a roll of anaglypta wallpaper.

Desperate for oxygen, we made one last futile stab at the airbrick before tipping ourselves down three flights of stairs and out into the raging kaleidoscope of colour and noise that is Hong Kong at night. On exiting the building we made a hasty and uninformed lane choice and found ourselves swept away in a swell of frail looking old women with iron hips who crushed our knees between their shopping baskets. In the chaos I detected a persistent tapping against my hip. A chicken, I noticed fleetingly, had attached itself to my leg. Its legs remained tied to the waist of a scary looking woman with a necklace of gulping fish garlanding her bosom. The chicken was swept away by the tide and we surged onward. I dedicated a fleeting moment of mourning to its glassy-eyed memory. A succession of appealing looking coffee shops flashed fleetingly into view. Armed only with impotent hand signals and a few limp bleating sounds, we failed to brake and helter past a cappuccino house at the speed of light. Something twanged ominously around my waist and I detected a vague loosening of vital undergarments. But this was no time for dress adjustment, the crowd surged on with a ferocious urgency scarily reminiscent of some of England's most memorable soccer fixtures. We passed a succession of Japanese department stores, their windows full of curiously small-headed mannequins, and a Marks and Spencers with all its solid British predictability and blazered, blue-rinsed customers.

We rounded a very tight corner, narrowly avoided a confrontation with a tram, and finally drew to a dishevelled and deflated stop outside a dubious looking cafe. I noted with disgruntlement that my belt had parted company from my trousers. Heavy with jet-lag and memories of the senseless packing frenzy that had filled our last few weeks, we dribbled pathetically into a cafe the colour of your worst decorating nightmare and order our dinner. This was our first night in Hong Kong and the journal that would chart our journey waited expectantly in my rucksack so far sullied only by an orange smear of coal tar soap. It was secreted away under our hotel room bed wedged between a cast iron waste-paper basket and a small pottery horse. Last minute farewell gifts, thoughtfully chosen by friends in the Japanese village I'd been living in for optimum portability, convenience, potential usefulness and kind of mass-to-volume ratio usually associated with small asteroids. Oh, I bleated, you really shouldn't have, relegating my Spartan little rucksack to hand baggage status as I hauled half-a-ton of traditional Japanese iron-ware onto my shoulder. The horse might help win favour with a difficult child but the waste-paper basket offered no obvious survival value in a transcontinental excursion that would take in Hong Kong, China, Outer Mongolia, Siberia, the Ukraine and Russia over the next thirty-one days. It reinforced my original and unchallenged theory that Japanese people just shouldn't travel.

The mystery of my missing belt was soon explained. Revived by some curiously red tea, our usual mindless optimism slunk back into view. With the same misplaced eagerness to culturally assimilate that had been our downfall during the time we'd just spent living in Japan, we embarked on the first of the many culinary adventures this trip would bring. While Laura delicately dunked her fingers in the watery Vietnamese soup, I merrily took my spoon to the finger bowl and started to drink. Things were fine until the waiters started laughing. They'd been menacing us with their brisk hand gestures and short hair cuts since we walked in with our water bottles and the fifteen rolls of toilet paper we'd picked up for a paltry sum at a local barbers. Apparently we lowered the general tone.

Laura, with her scattering of indispensable Chinese characters, had steered me towards a dish which she confidently identified as fish. I had my suspicions the moment it arrived. If this was a fish then natural selection was surely a cruel and vicious hoax perpetrated by an eccentric sailor with a penchant for flightless birds and small hunting dogs. Stringy and black, with the faintest hint of Moroccan tanning oil - I was confident that we had solved the mystery of my missing belt. The waiter, after a moment's confusion, resurfaced with a small dictionary. He thumbed painfully through the pages before proclaiming his verdict with a serious face. "Tendon" he proclaimed gravely. "Cow? Cow tendon?" squeaked Laura hopefully, her eyes closed as if medication might actually help. "No cow. Dog," he announced with a proud grin that displayed a fascinating gap in his teeth. I delicately laid my chopsticks down at the side of my dish. Enough assimilation for one night, my eyes pleaded at Laura over the table. Mildly disillusioned with our first night on the streets of Hong Kong, we headed back through the streets towards our airless, windowless, characterless cabin. There we gravely embarked on a grisly and interminable laundry saga that would introduce my one pair of socks to seventeen different brands of local washing-powder in the course of the next 68 days.

I COULD HEAR MY FATHER SAY: YOU GAVE YOUR PASSPORTS TO WHO????

The next day, the first real day of our holiday, we awoke with the thirst for adventure and air raging in our throats. The macabre culinary adventures of the previous night were immortalised only in the small stack of empty toilet rolls in the bathroom. Considering the fact that the tendon seemed impossible to digest I doubted Laura's theory that her first bout of diarrhoea was exclusively ligament-induced. Nevertheless, I couldn't help marvelling at the fortitude of her digestive enzymes.

Today's goal was to procure tickets for our upcoming trip across Siberia on the trans-Siberian express. From the sanitary sanctuary of my flat in Japan I had communicated very efficiently with a Mancunian called Mark who had apathetically bothered himself with making the preliminary arrangements for our trip. He hung out in a flat in Nathan Road, the heart of the old colonial centre of Hong Kong, in a dilapidated building grandly named the Chung King Mansions. Mark greeted us with a disinterested hum and a vaguely disguised mumble about London woosies which made us think momentarily about taking our business elsewhere. Fortunately, just in time, we remembered that Mark's impenetrable smugness was probably rooted in his Mancunian blood and the fact that as self-anointed "Emperor of the Siberian Railway" he boasted a complete monopoly on all Trans-Siberian Rail tickets sold in Hong Kong. Out tongues were duly bitten.

Mark's office was disturbingly womb like, with walls shrouded in furry pink banners and blankets and a motley assortment of disreputable looking cats stapled to the sofa. There was a paranoid glint in their eyes, as if they were aware of the precariousness of their continued existence in this city, and we were careful not to turn our backs on them. Mark was a hunkering football-playing kind of chap with an unusually small head. Despite this, we willingly handed him our credit cards and passports and a couple of blank cheques, in retrospect a little rash, but the omnipotence of travel gave us an invincible feeling. He popped them into his jacket pocket between a stick of celery and a vintage party popper and gave us each a puce-coloured "We did the Trans-Siberian T-shirt" to compensate us for the indefinite confiscation of our entire bureaucratic identifies.

About an hour later, as we dined on a dish that regrettably contained the word "gizzard" (we had yet to conclusively establish what a gizzard was - Laura hedged hopefully towards something oesophageal while I remained haunted by stills from an X-rated black and white movie I'd once seen in Russia), we began to question our mindless naiveté. Mark held all evidence of our futile earthly existence in his jacket pocket. It was just a matter of time before we whipped ourselves up into a delirious frenzy of paranoia. I think we started to cry somewhere around the time we got back to Chung King Mansions to find a sign on Mark's door saying "Back Monday". It was only Friday night.

We spent the rest of the morning hunting down people who looked like us (there were few in Hong Kong). Our theory went along the lines that if someone bought our pilfered passports they were likely to try and change their appearance to look like us. It was a long shot and one that won us some fairly acrid scowls from the people we stalked through department stores and into public toilets (mostly   women's though I found a long-lost twin in a young Taiwanese man in a mackintosh). Around two o'clock we realised there was nothing we could do until Sunday and so decided to invest the remainder of our day in an orgy of shopping, fine dining and something that would have been utterly unthinkable had it not been for our recent trauma. Yes, we visited one of those peculiarly misplaced institutions, with all its tacky "authenticities" and annoying Irish barmen - the English pub abroad. Designed as crutches for feeble-minded ex-pats whose delicate colonial constitutions couldn't stomach the thought of being in a foreign country, these atrocities housed a pathetic scattering of displaced souls. The ubiquitous Irish barman ("taking a year out mate!") was gratifyingly replaced by an annoying kiwi called Les who was something of an authority on Chinese culture and customs despite spending twenty-four hours a day in the basement cell they called "The Mad Dogs". Given Les, the darkness of the pub and its similarities to our airless bedsit I could well understand why the dogs might choose insanity over sobriety.

YOU NEED TOILET?
THIS WATERMELON SHOULD HELP!

That evening we headed to the market area of Temple Street where it seemed the whole of Hong Kong congregated by night to hawk and trade and pawn. The guide-book's timid rhetoric had not prepared us for the explosion of colours and smells and sounds that greeted us as we came up from the Jordan subway. Old men with bowed legs ripped the tops off Fanta bottles with their toothless gums and spat them into the streets. In a makeshift stall across from the Wilson Car Park, men in strangely tight dresses wailed alarmingly at a bemused looking crowd while making curiously effeminate hand gestures. It was an alarming chorus, high-pitched and nail gratingly off-key. The hand gestures were all rather sinister and we were very careful to look away during the chorus (distinguished from the main song by its irritating repetitiveness and unearthly intensity). An orchestra populated by elderly men playing instruments fresh from the set of some surrealist fantasy drama provided a curious breed of harmony from their seats behind the mewling men. Confused, we wondered if this was some kind of open-air criminal investigation. Laura speculated with misplaced excitement that they might be eunuchs. The young man next to us overheard and apologetically explained that these men were amateur opera-singers providing (and I swear this was the word he used) *entertainment.* We moved swiftly on.

As we walked on, dapper young men in tight tee-shirts hawked silks in a catalogue of colours under neon signs that blazed their unnecessary advertisements in a kaleidoscope of pinks and yellows. We came to a street lit almost entirely with small lanterns dangling over stalls where men (usually elderly) greeted rows of patiently waiting clients. These were fortune tellers, ready to read faces or palms and reveal past lives and the future. One boasted, in accord with the changing times "advice for nice home and good career after emigration". Another offered advice on past, present and future "lice". An alarming thought.

Further along we passed nuts and fruits and dismembered animals painted red and speared on spits, a britallion of wristwatches glinting in the pink-purple light, radios by the ship-load, stacked stories high; monstrous, swollen, gleaming fruits bursting open on the pavements. Fresh from the stifling homogeny and self-consciousness of Japan's city slickers the sense of chaos that permeated the market was refreshing. People went about their daily business seemingly untroubled by the bizarre and eccentric sights that surrounded them. We saw few of the twitchy little insinuations that seemed to zap between people in the streets of Japan where people always seemed desperate for the fickle approval of strangers in subways and clerks in hotel lobbies. Hong Kong at night seemed to an outrageous, even vulgar carnival of the bizarre, the perverse and the simply unexpected. Intoxicated by this apparent and un-self-conscious madness, we wandered dreamily through the streets, absorbing the colours, the sights, the smells, the sounds.

Until the toilet crisis struck. No one could have predicted the urgency with which the need gripped me. I was rapidly losing faith in Laura's random scattering of a few arty Chinese characters and in desperation resorted to sign-language. My euphemistic hand-washing gestures were answered twice by old women offering small bowls of water in which to wash my hands, once by a man bearing a very ripe water-melon and twice by small children proffering chickens. I started to run. Just as feelings like labour pangs started to tear through me, we were rescued by a dapper young man in an smart white uniform. He abducted us through a garbage-rimmed doorway which opened into a huge metal staircase, spiralling up and down into the darkness. There were no lights, and we could make out only his white gloves gesturing at us in the darkness. At the top of the stairs he led us through a door into a large black room that seemed to be flashing. The sound of gunfire reverberated around the room. We dropped to our knees. At the moment of impact I realised that the shock could only be bad for my bowels. As our eyes adjusted to the dark, the realisation stole over us that we were in a movie theatre, silhouetted against a big-screen re-run of an old Jackie Chan film. The man in white was an usher. Mortified as two thousand eyes seemed to leak out of the darkness, we crept on hands and knees across the whole front of the cinema. Our heads practically brushed the knees of the people in the front row who seemed suspicious of this unaccustomed intimacy during a PG rated feature presentation. One old man tried to stroke my hair but this was no time to stop and make small talk. The usher, who entered into the subterfuge with his white gloves and Mission-Impossible-style coolness, led us out through another door, down three more flights of stairs and finally, finally, finally, into a toilet, where I could liberate myself in the luxury of an air-conditioned cubicle. When I finally emerged, pale and wan and shaking from the over aggressive air-conditioning, Laura was muttering grimly to herself about the revenge of the tendon. I took solace from the fact that none of the canine ligament could possibly have survived my recent purge.

NO GIZZARDS PLEASE - WE'RE BRITISH

We finished the night with a very sophisticated dining experience in one of Hong Kong's "nicest" eating establishments, proudly called The Noble Restaurant. The waitress, in full diamante cocktail regalia, glared as we battled in with our water bottles and the fifteen rolls of toilet paper we'd picked up for a paltry sum at a local barbers. We were left in no doubt that the tone plummeted on our entry. From that moment on our table was surreptitiously stalked by a battalion of short men in dinner jackets. Compensating very obviously for our scruffy demeanour, we splashed out on a whole Peking Duck, complete with all the trimmings. The noble bird was served, (disconcertingly with its head and wings and feet still attached) - along with a soup containing a generous scattering of entrails and indispensable bodily organs. The waiter sneeringly confirmed our worst suspicions - there was a gizzard in there too. Strategically positioned in the middle of the table, the plump-breasted bird looked mournfully up at us from his frilly nest of doilies and silverware. I doubted that such an elegant ruff would compensate him for the indignity of his present predicament. We tried turning him round but the rear aspect was even less appetising. The more we studied him from every angle, the more we felt we knew him. Eventually we had to call for reinforcements to help us carve. Laura was already teetering on a delicate neural tightrope and the prospect of butchering a defenceless chicken might very well have pushed her over the edge.

Our walk home took us along the edge of Hong Kong's famous Victoria harbour, where daring couples teased each other under the green glow of the pawnbrokers lamps. Christmas tree buildings stretching into the blackness made a handsome backdrop for the spectacular display of harbour lights picked out in the velvety waters. It was hard not to feel awed by the colossal scale of the harbour. I was proudly and claustrophobically overwhelmed by this display of civil engineering and architectural might and wondered if there was anywhere else in the world where man had so conspicuously shaped the skyline. New York perhaps, San Francisco.....Emboldened by a new appreciation of the futility of our existence in the scale of human accomplishment, we made our way laughingly over to a small child blowing bubbles along the harbour's edge. I always considered I was a natural with children and was confident that the little boy would let me join in his game. The little git kicked me hard in the shins before wiping bubble juice all over my new silk shirt. He hurled me a nice fat raspberry before buggering off into the darkness. I saw the edge of the harbour close by and momentarily wished for the unthinkable. Laura was fittingly scathing about my misplaced trust in the innocence of children and passed me a piece of toilet paper (we had some to spare) to wipe down my shirt. It was time to go home.

MANY FOREIGNER NOT LIKE CAT DUMPLING

This morning's goal was a small cafe in a little alley called Bird Street. The guide book had waxed lyrical in its patronising way about the charm of this unaffected cafe and our appetites were whetted for a taste of "Real China". Bird Street cowered shyly in the belly of a catacomb of narrow streets and alleyways behind a maze of old market-places. The colour went from the air as we delved into the bowels of

Hong Kong's oldest quarters. This was a world of yellow walls and old cobbled streets, open drains and the crumbling remains of old walled courtyards and gardens now seeded with market stalls and fringed with old wooden houses. Here children carved chairs and pipes from spindles of willow and birch and played chequers on the side of the street. White-bearded men in mandarin collars carved intricate bird-cages from bamboo in the shadow of candles that stretched up to catch a glimpse of the big blue sky; the smell of cedarwood and stewed green tea permeated the dusty streets, mingling with the tang of spices and bonfires. Stalls were stacked high with delicate porcelain water bowls and multi-storey bamboo cages that resembled some of Hong Kong's sadder high -rises. On every corner a new face followed us behind a shroud of tobacco smoke and incense, silent and watching, hands clasped under a white-haired chin on the top of a bamboo cane. We were offered parrots, chickens (ten to a net bag, still clucking), tea, calligraphy inks, pipes, and a sad-looking slab of Kendal mint cake, the origin and authenticity of which had to be doubted. We hurried purposefully through the maze of streets, feeling desperately gung-ho in this sinister Chinese underworld that we populated in our minds with warlords and gangsters. Secretly we were both excited by the prospect of meeting Michael Palin in one of these ochre-walled back streets.

Following Murphy's law of travel, the cafe we were heading for became more and more elusive the closer we got. Out natural geographical dyslexia was compounded by the fact that we had not one jot of functional Chinese between us. Mockingly indulgent as people were when we flagged them down to entertain them with our impressive repertoire of obscene hand gestures, we didn't seem to get our point across: inevitably, things deteriorated to the point where a rough impression of a chicken and a lot of tweeting were our last resort. It was all getting very humiliating when Laura unleashed a loud cry and began gesturing up at a window three stories up There, hanging calmly in the window, rocking gently in the early-morning smog, must have been a hundred bird cages.

The scene in the cafe was surreal, one, maybe two hundred men of all ages sitting drinking tea, reading the papers and playing chess. Each man had carried a caged bird to the cafe with him, and while the men sipped and gulped and spat, the birds chirped and sang in their little gilt prisons. Conspicuous in hiking boots and appalling Japanese trousers, we slunk into a corner by the men's toilets (there was no women's toilet). The proprietor advanced with a sceptical frown. Anxious to assimilate, we gestured at a fat pile of dumplings on the table next to us and raised a hesitant single finger. As we waited for our feast of uncertain origin to materialise, we stole hesitant glances around us. There was a serenity in this quiet gathering of man and birds that few places have held onto, and we were both glad we'd come here.

Our dumplings were delivered fifteen minutes later. The waiter dropped them off at arms length (we later learnt that all Europeans smell of dairy products) with a sly, but challenging, sideways glance. He then retreated to a safe distance and with that lack of self-consciousness peculiarly common to the Chinese people leant back against a wall with fifteen friends to watch us dine. Performance anxiety made precision chopstick manipulation difficult but we persevered. Halfway through her third dumpling, Laura let out a little cry, and, recovering nicely under the circumstances, delicately fished out a small pointed tooth of uncertain animal origin. She recited under her breath the mantra for gastronomic survival we'd developed in Japan -

"Don't think about it, don't think about it, don't think about it"......and carried on chewing with a pained expression on her face. Several minutes later the waiter approached us. "You like?" he smirked, with a confident backwards glance at his friends. "Yes, very nice" we gargled through mouthfuls. "Many foreigner not like this dish" he observed grimly, nodding his head to emphasise his point. "Oh?" Voices trembling as we waited for the inevitable. "Yes, they no like cat dumpling." Thank you for sharing, we whispered inside our heads, laying down our chopsticks. "Ve-ry fu-ull" I finally said, with exaggerated pointing to my belly. Just once, I thought, I would like to finish my meal before finding out what it was.

We left the beautiful cafe with its twinkling music and headed back out into the streets. We headed back through the maze of markets with what turned out to be a misplaced sense of intuition. Hopelessly lost and mapless, ten minutes later, we found ourselves in a macrocosm of the beautiful bird cafe, a market clamouring and clattering with men of all ages buying and selling and admiring what must have been half of Asia's bird population. Warblers and finches and tiny striped sparrows that fluttered like delicate porcelain toys, handpainted with the greatest care with a magic brush, in their gilded cages. The sound was unearthly, and chilling memories of Alfred Hitchcock's famous film came flooding back. Laura put a newspaper on her head for no particular reason. She disliked, apparently, their general fluttering. It seemed that this was somewhere people came to trade, and maybe to show, their birds: evidently it fulfilled a social function too for everywhere we looked people huddled together in little gaggles, discussing birds or sharing a newspaper with a dusty mist of bird fluff and wheat husks raining down on their shoulders.

I LIKE CARROTS, I LIKE POTATOES, I LIKE PEPPERS, I LIKE...

We found ourselves next in a place called Aberdeen, where we were approached by a charmingly persistent sampan lady who wanted us to ride on her boat. Normally shy of organised excursions, we were intrigued by her promise that this trip would be different and so found ourselves on a small wooden fishing boat amply draped in blue tarpaulin and decorated at all key joints with three inch long staples. The boat turned out of the harbour and along a stretch of river for a little while before emptying into a muddy brown harbour which we were told was a typhoon shelter. We saw a hundred, maybe two, squat wooden boats, each circled by a wide wooden-slatted deck on which whole families washed and cooked and slept and ate. Washing lines circled each deck, trousers and shirts trumpeting as the wind flared through them and smoke from cooking fires swilled over them. People hurdled between the boats, always seeming to be carrying something that tied up one hand while they scaled the system of ropes and ladders and railings that decorated each boat. Toddlers veered perilously close to the edge of the boats, men mending fishing nets offering admonishing barks to ward them off the side. Our guide told us how just a few years ago, mothers would strap empty gourds to their children's backs like little life vests in case of calamity. These were house-boats, and the people who lived in them were Vietnamese refugees, many of whom had lived here for ten to twenty years. Apparently the number of people living here had diminished to a small fraction of the number of families living here in the 1970s. Many of the "boat people" had been resettled from their bobbing waterfront sampans into high rise blocks of flats that sprung up in architectural isolation from the quaint harbourfront surroundings. The straggling remnants of this once-thriving boat community seemed strangely untouched by the hard pace and bustle of the commercial sector, or the cut-throat opulence of the international hospitality set. The people on the boats watched us with caution, or perhaps mockery - contempt for our narrow lives that made us pay to steal a glance of the real world through our expensive camera lenses. And how did we look at them? With embarrassment perhaps, laced with guilt, because we'd chosen to make the temporary experiment of being nomads, homeless. With a rose-tinted over-romanticisation of their water-borne, sunset-washed lifestyle? With the morbid curiosity of spectators at a side-show fair, anonymity making us bold and rude as we stared into their homes and lives?.

After the old motor boat spluttered into the harbour and drew herself to a dignified halt, a group of teenage boys swept up in their boat and offered us a trip round the harbour to watch the sun set. I seized the opportunity to practice my faltering Cantonese on the young man sitting next to me. He swallowed hard and appeared to be concentrating very hard on what I was saying. While I grappled with the dangerous intonations that can, with a slight twist, throw an innocent sentence off the Cliff of Obscenity, he chewed thoughtfully on a piece of straw. By now I had told him how much I liked vegetables (cleverly substituting seven different vegetable words one after the other into my sentence)., but I sensed I needed more to hold his interest. I bravely threw in a few adjectives, adding a whole new dimension to our discourse. Now I could tell him how I liked big marrows, round potatoes and many more favourites, adding supplementary hand gestures where appropriate. As the sun settled down in the sky, I experimented with changing like to love, vegetables to fruits, and I to "do you?". There was nothing to this conversation lark.

While I discoursed at length on the merits of red apples versus blue carrots, Junk ships with their billowing graceful sails started to materialise from the amber half-light like ghosts, trawling the muddy waters with an eerie stillness, despite their speed, and a silence that somehow seemed louder than the sound of our own rattling motor-boat. The scene was too complete, too perfect, to insult by reducing it to a six by four print so our cameras stayed locked away in their cases. Awe-struck, I stopped drilling the poor boy next to me about fresh produce and we committed the picture, with the utmost reverence, to our memory. The boat eventually drew to a spluttering standstill by the harbour wall. We offered the boys our profoundest thanks in squeaky textbook Cantonese. A man standing on the waterfront called out "They Vietnamese people, no Chinese, no speak Chinese......". I was sure I could hear him say "stupid" in muttered tones as his sentence trailed to a stop.

ONE LUMP OR TWO IN YOUR COFFEE?

Our last but one day in Hong Kong, and yet yearnings for the little village I'd left behind in Japan weighed on my mind. I was not designed for company today, and Laura and I solemnly parted company at 9.00 o'clock, arranging to meet again at 4.00 p.m.

Thinking a walk through the markets would stimulate my senses and rouse me from the sticky reverie I seemed to be trapped in, I took a tram to Pottenger Lane, an older part of Hong Kong where the guide books promised a total titillation of the senses. It certainly was.

The markets were was a throbbing blaze of colour and sound. Each stall emitted its own smells, sights and sounds, it was the full sensory package, grotesque but compelling. With every step further into the markets I wanted to get up and walk away, but a sick curiosity to find out what lay around the next corner kept me moving like a zombie further and further into the bowels of this world. It was like some hideous zoo, almost every animal known to man had a starring role in this ghastly carnival of death, each breed its own peculiar death cry, its own trumpet of pain, its own look of confusion. The black-eyed heads of hundreds of chickens protruding at dislocated angles from the constricting squares of their chicken-wire cages. Legs, just legs, hanging undecorously from stiff wires like rows of tombstones, huge indolent fishy slabs the colour of satsumas trawling through a puddle of water just two inches deep, plucked and sliced while still alive and quivering on the metal chopping board, if the price is right. Cages heaving, almost imperceptibly with the slow, squishy movements of toads, a vat of steaming water brooding ominously next to them, ready for a convenient lunchtime dip. Pharmacists' stalls with huge glass Ali Baba jars swollen with ginger and ginseng and roots, deer antlers, snakes, and at the top of the stall, out of the reach of prying paws, tiger penis, that notorious aphrodisiac. Racks and racks of live snakes, impaled at one end on a skewer, gyrate through their death throws as the coals beneath them start to glow, lizards blackened and charred leave pathetic wormy trails of soot on the glass as they struggle to climb the impossible glass walls of their final prison.

At the end of the market, shallow granite steps ringed with haberdashery stalls led like a ladder up onto Pottenger street, its spiralling path marked by beautiful red lanterns every few steps. Here the backstreet world of Pottenger market seemed to recede into the swirling mists of some half-remembered dream, and as I ploughed back into the normal streets with their normal sights and sounds, it seemed that the world had suddenly lost a dimension. As I tottered off, with wobbling knees and a swelling sense of sickness in my gizzard, to meet Laura, I remembered that I'd wanted some time to myself that morning. Now I couldn't wait to see her!

We headed that afternoon to the western side of Hong Kong, starting accidentally with an inconspicuous but thriving community called Kennedy. We were quite disappointed with the lack of plausibly Chinese-sounding place names in Hong Kong. It was as if the plan of those xenophobic colonials had been to eradicate once and for all, any taint of Chinese-ness from the colony just as one would pledge to eradicate a fishy smell from a suspiciously stinky ice-box. Kennedy was a kaleidoscope of a place, in every direction a vignette of working life in this secluded neighbourhood unfolded, strained looking mothers towing lines of pink-cheeked children in drunken squabbling rows; unlikely items, carcasses, washing machines, baskets flapping with chickens, sacks of freshly laundered clothes sweet with the smell of rice starch and jasmine being emptied into the litter-speckled streets from the backs of trucks. Spice stalls warmed the air with pungent orange smells that made you think of all the places you ever wanted to visit. Chickens in various stages of dismemberment cowered helplessly in bamboo cages. Down a back street shops fronted by huge coil upon huge coil of tightly wound steel cable announced unnecessarily that they sold steel cable. It was if they were compelled to boast of their nautical connections. In a market hall, flapping fish, heads turning this way and that, writhed open-mouthed and gasping in consternation as if retelling, breathless with excitement, how some epic race was won or some small child plucked from harm. They appear slightly less boastful of their maritime beginnings, more mindful of their pending and inauspicious end on that cold metal table. We declined to partake of the small samples proffered from the blackened hands of the fish-sellers, preferring instead to seek a cool sanctuary in someplace vegetarian..

We found a cafe in one the backstreets that promised real Kona coffee. Of sorts. The sugar cubes were yellow with fat mosquitoes vitrified in the congealed crystals. The cafe was painted the deepest purple with furry tablecloths and dark lighting that merged perfectly with the rest of our nightmares. A man approached us from the shadows and greeted us in perfect English. He asked us what we'd seen so far in Canton and I mentioned the markets. He laughed politely at the expression on my face. "We Chinese find it funny that you eat the cow and the pig who help you in the fields and bring in your family harvest and yet you are so sentimental over the cat and the dog". "You eat cow and pig too" I said, thinking of the piglets we'd seen struggling in tiny mesh baskets around people's necks and handlebars. "In the villages", he said "the people worship the pig and the cow. It is just in the city, where people no longer worry about the harvest, that we enjoy the luxury of eating the pig and the cow". By now I felt as if The Pig and The Cow warranted capital letters, an invitation to close family gatherings and exclusive use of my Diner's card. But I had to see his point. I flicked a yellow sugar cube across the table hoping to dislodge a tenacious mosquito from its crusty corner. The waiter gave me a disappointed look and hurried back to the kitchens.

THE OLD WALLED CITY

The day finished with a trip to see the old walled city, billed dramatically as Hong Kong's most notorious pocket of vice and squalor. Originally established in the pre-British days as a quaint Chinese military outpost, the enclave was immediately walled up by the fastidious Brits and carefully forgotten about, so carefully in fact that when the 1898 New Territories lease was drawn up, no provision was made for the Walled City, leaving the enclave ambiguously uncontrolled. During the Japanese occupation that original granite wall was torn down and, with later, with touching disregard for sentiment, buried under concrete to form the new airport runway at Kai Tai. After the war, the Walled City became home to a disreputable scattering of China's vilest and most perverse emigrants, " a cesspool of iniquity, with heroin divans, brothels and all things unsavoury" to coin the words of the despondent Governor Alexander Grantham, who sounds a miserable kind of chap. In the minds of the fastidious British occupiers, it was a seething underworld that offered a hellish, lightless, airless existence to the scum who had to live there. Not that they were bothered enough to improve conditions, more rankled that it continued to survive as a kind of festering sore on the otherwise unruffled bottom of this orderly British colony. Its reputation (and the overwhelming smell of fish - the City produced over 80% of the colony's fish balls) kept the prim-nosed Brits away and the very real community of the Walled City eked out its furtive existence, complete with all the usual trappings of family, and work and religion and survival, behind doors that were all but marked with red crosses.

When we finally arrived, after a succession of scary public transport experiences, we discovered to our chagrin that most of the older buildings had actually been pulled down in the 1930s and that only a smattering of old houses and slum-style corrugated iron dwellings clung to life in this no man's zone. Some 30,000 people had been, or were in the process of being, relocated to austere high-rises in the city. An old man who guarded the gateway to the old city hawked chestnuts from a small stove that his son poked determinedly in the sweltering afternoon heat. His son told us who people were reported to be dying from too much space in the narrow high-rises with their deafening views that showed patches of the big blue sky. I looked up at the pregnant rain clouds and admired his whimsical Chinese optimism. The plan, he told us, was to demolish the rest of the Walled City and build a park where high flying executives could walk their snooty dogs. He told us with a despondent shake of his head that he hoped they'd turn it into a playground for children, or a big tea house selling a hundred kinds of dumplings. He didn't seem hopeful, as if its eventual complete obliteration and an influx of suited rottweillers were a regrettable, but inevitable conclusion to the tale of the Walled City. We left him reflecting sombrely and dripping sweat all over the chestnuts. All that we could really see of the old Walled City were a few bitten off stubs of granite where the old buildings had been hacked down, and a scattering of iron roofed huts strewn about as if dropped from a passing aeroplane and left to seed on the dead soil. We hung around for a little while before returning home in a sad mood to share a stale mars-bar and half a cup of plastic coffee. Darkness found us gasping for air in our bug-infested beds wondering without a trace of sentiment if part of that airless, lightless spirit persisted somewhere in our chocolate-coloured hotel room.

A BRUSH WITH BUREAUCRACY

The morning began with the long-anticipated trip to retrieve our passports from Mark. He greeted our frantic knocks with a bemused and unnecessarily hostile bleariness (it <u>was</u> almost 7.00 am) and told us to come back later. We tried to utilise the principles of non-violent resistance to stage a small sit-in on his step but he closed the door and the gesture was lost. Now we knew he was back in town but were yet to see our passports. We stood outside his apartment for about an hour trying to psyche him out by staring aggressively at his curtains but he didn't come back to the door. I found some consolation picturing him sticking pins under his nails and rocking on his heels with his back to the curtains saying "I won't let them get to me, I won't let them.....". The alternative scenario was that he was frantically packing his bags and getting ready to leave the country. Anyway our protest had been disappointingly limp; besides which we were starting to look a little obsessive. A gaggle of concerned local residents had started to surround us. All we could do was come back later.

After a nail-biting breakfast of coffee and .... nails..... we headed back to Mark's place. It was now nearly nine o'clock. This time his yellow door loyally heroically absorbed our limp-fisted battering; its sad-looking letter-box mouth not even twisting up at the corners as we poundered and hammered and thumped. No one came to the door, irate or otherwise. Panicing now, we hammered and hammered and hammered until a man with a mop hunkered over and pressed the door-bell in an annoying casual way. There was a little smirk in there too. Now Mark came to the door, still not excited to see us but as least he invited us in. The trip was brief (he was in no mood for conversation) but we didn't care. Happily reunited with our passports, now bearing the Russian visas Mark had mysteriously procured over the weekend (interestingly our passports returned with pencil scribblings in almost every margin - I flicked them really quickly to see if they'd drawn a little man in various stages of jumping up and down but the scribbles remained a mystery), we optimistically allocated the rest of the morning to securing our Chinese visas. Time was running out, we were due to leave Hong Kong in two days and we still had no legitimate way of entering China. An official at the Hong Kong Travel Bureau cheerfully assured us that as a last resort Mr Bribery and Mrs Corruption would happily escort us over the waters. His annoying use of cute-isms made our worries no less palpable.

The Chinese Embassy, which had now been closed for five days for no particular reason, was, predictably, closed. The rash of red characters which danced on the door meant nothing to us, but we took a gamble and decided to wait. Someone had told us the visa office sometimes opened in the afternoon for short periods. Sure enough, at about three o'clock, the doors cranked open and a sleepy looking man in a smart green uniform materialised in the doorway. (He seemed surprised himself). As we meandered to our feet with an "its all in the bag now" kind of smugness, sixty-seven people carrying a miscellany of household objects (including a large vase, two chickens, a scattering of briefcases, several rucksacks and a kitten) barged right past us. It was quite a stunning display of athleticism. Resigned to another interminable wait, we took up the sixty eighth and ninth places in the queue.

After about an hour, the dumplings and the tea began to catch up with me. The immigration toilets were closed to visitors, I was firmly informed. I had no choice but to seek satisfaction outside the arms of Comrade Mao and took an urgent jog along the harbourside. The first place I came to was the ostentatious Grand Hyatt hotel, a monstrous gilt-encrusted chandelier of a hotel. The lobby, decked out in art deco opulence in the style of a 1930's cruise ship was stuffed full of black-suited businessmen talking loudly over the limp trickle of pan pipes playing favourite TV theme tunes. The solid black marble doors bound grandly in brass looked sternly at me. I attached myself unconvincingly to a party of Spanish metallurgists but it was just a question of time before the burly doorman escorted me back out to the street with a disdainful glance at my flip-flops. To my incredible delight I found myself facing a Dunkin Donuts. While Laura sweated and hauled our backpacks an inch an hour along immigration's millipedic conveyor belt, I dined on coffee and donuts and relieved myself at leisure in cubicle that smelt of dettox.

Returning forty minutes later with a limp donut for Laura, I found we had jumped far ahead and were just hours away from our first brush with the gophers of Chinese officialdom. A nervous tension bordering on hysteria began to mount. If our visas were denied, the rest of our trip was condemned to a wistful stroke in our imagination. We were due to board the Trans-Siberian express in Beijing and the rest of our journey across Siberia to Russia and then back to England was carefully mapped out and paid for. This had to go well. Things were not looking good. Several young men with pony tails and CND badges had left looking very despondent and a young girl from somewhere in Eastern Europe had broken down in tears right in front of us. Laura dismantled her my pony tail and I struggled to make my eyebrows look less prominent. There was no telling what would do it for these guys.

Sometime around five o'clock we finally faced the man who could completely destroy our trip. We put on our best girl faces as he handed us a sheaf of papers to complete. All the people behind us in the queue were dismissed and told to come back tomorrow. Sweat trickled down the back of our necks as they scrutinised our documents with microscopic precision. They asked for signatures, queried our addresses, inspected our passports and took a close look at Laura's watch. And then, just as we gave up hope of ever seeing Lenin, they stamped our passports, stapled up our papers, and bid us be gone with an officious hand-gesture. As we stumbled down the steps into the sweltering afternoon heat, we couldn't help but grin. We were on our way to China!

FIVE HUNDRED YEARS OF
SEXUAL REPRESSION...

Wild with relief (never a pleasant state to be in), and assured that we were to do some "real travelling" in China, we relaxed our quest for cultural immersion and struck a course across the city to the starting point of The Peak Tram, Hong Kong's notorious tourist-puller. In the heydays of colonial rule, Hong Kong's sweaty, bulbous faced elite would endure the arduous three-hour ascent of the peak to escape the general heat and gunge of Hong Kong's notoriously humid summers to languish in ostentatious mansions whimsically named Brockhurst and Abergeldie in the best Colonial tradition. Apparently the small army of Chinese men who hauled them up the Peak in hammock-like contraptions also found the excursions a little inconvenient but the Surgeon General's evangelical exhortations to enjoy the Peak's salubrious air could not be ignored. The advent of The Tram in 1888 and its eight- minute ascent lessened the load of coolies and colonials alike and opened up whole new commuter route from the Peak down to the Hong Kong's Central district.

The Tram scours a monumental gash up the side of Victoria Peak, defying gravity with its almost vertical ascent (the steepest funicular railway in the world, we had been proudly assured by our landlady). Unnerved by a shiny faced photographer who hung out of the tram at suicidal angles to get the best shots of his balloon -wielding children, we kept our eyes on the bay. A hundred emerald islands floated in the turquoise waters, each ringed by its own milky beaches and a halo of jade green where the beaches shelved down under the shallow sea. It had been dark when we flew in and I had no sense at all of the richness of the seas in this part of the world. In the harbour a hundred boats waited in tidy rows for the start of their journey. From the peak we could see them, fishing boats, passenger ferries, liners and junk ships with their flapping sails and sturdy beams trawling through the mossy waters, a world of criss-crossing journeys and lives that glimpsed each other over the swell of the seas and the stern of a boat. And the brooding bulk of Hong Kong, the hub of this eternal cycle of arrivals and departures, sat queenly on her emerald green throne and watched the seas spin around her.

We embarked optimistically on a little stroll around the peak. Rhododendron, bamboo, jasmine and giant palms shimmered along our path, wetting our noses with the musty bitterness of moss and rotting forest floors. As we circled the Peak the uninhabited southern slopes of the island swung into view stretching down past Pakfulam Reservoir, backed by a canvas of power plants and industrial facilities. At the junction of the Harlech and Lugard roads, we headed west towards the slopes of Sai Ho Shan, a bare, wind-scraped mountain on a track that no one else seemed to be taking. The scramble to the summit was sharp and nail-grinding, but our reward, a deafening silence streaked only with the bleating murmur of ships horns bellowing down in the azure waters floating up to swirl around our mountain-top watchpoint.

Heading back down to our original path we continued our encirclement of Victoria Peak, creeping now upon an other-world-ish mountain-top community where obscenely opulent houses languished idly in the oppressive heat, blinds and shutters clamped shut like the fluttering eyelids of some delicate colonial woman with a wobbly constitution. I had heard that Hong Kong boasted the highest number of Rolls Royce's per capita of any place in the world and suspected that they were all stowed up here in jewel encrusted garages. Many of our Japanese friends had warned us in grim whispers of the compulsive, unrelenting avarice of the Chinese cousins over the Pacific that they regarded with a fragile mixture of contempt and jealousy. The Japanese I knew seemed to see Hong Kong as some kind of hedonistic underworld where the feudal trappings of history and filial obligation were blithely disregarded and the shackles of 5000 years of sexual repression just cast aside. Envy mixed reluctantly with reproach in their voices. Hong Kong was one of the few Pacific-Rim countries where material recovery from the deprivation of wartime rivalled that of Japan, except that in Hong Kong the ostentatious exhibition of material wealth was applauded. My friend Mr Takahashi could not disguise his delight that the debaucherous island was being turned over to its puritanical parent over the water. "Then things will have to calm down there" he admonished with authority and a thinly veiled sense of "_na_ na na _na_ na". I wondered if indeed, the prodigal sheep would return to the flock, patched up and limping slightly but submitting itself humbly for rehabilitation in the best communist tradition. We would have to wait and see.

Later that evening we had the chance to ask an old man in a curious polyester smock what he thought about the return to Chinese rule. He had studied in Japan in the 1930s and still remembered some of the Japanese he'd learnt then. He imparted his comments with a military bark that had Laura running for the tram. "I was a nationalist, so I worked against the communists. I have been safe here, but now they will find me. I will have to move to America, maybe, or Canada to escape the communist dogs". (He used the Japanese word for Beagle, which made the communist threat seem a lot less menacing). We tried to ask him more questions but he was in a hurry and dismissed us with an imperious nod of his head and a flash of a shy smile. Many Chinese had fled to Hong Kong in the years during Mao TseTung's ascent from an eccentric yokel with a penchant for horsehair to the leader of a quarter of the world's population. Siding with the paranoid militarist Chiang Kai Shek who in the true spirit of social reform hated all poor people, many of the industrialists and land-owners, and those who had been contaminated by exposure to the West (with its hedonistic ideas and obsession with hair removal) fled to Hong Kong. Now they feared, like Mr Li, that a return to horse-hair was imminent.

Our expectations of China were still ill-formed, gathered as they were from our adolescent exposure to Karate Kid movies, and Xena

The Warrior Princess' ongoing tussles with exotic Mandarin warlords. They largely featured gangs and opium and ladies in fox-fur stoles and shockingly red lipstick. Of communism and the communist way, we knew, and had seen, little. A businessman who had overheard our conversation with Mr Li offered his opinion. "There will be no trade, no free enterprise, once the Chinese take Hong Kong back. They will suffocate the business spirit of Hong Kong, the pulse of her financial heart - " he beat his fist against his breast to emphasise the tragedy and hopelessness of it all - "we will all die poor men". His friend nudged him. "But think of the women. All looking for rich husbands". Our friend was not to be consoled. "Peasants. Women in China get no education. They know nothing about running a business". "But they will stay at home and make us coffee and bring it to us in bed..." His friend was getting quite excited. Wondering what would happen to Hong Kong, we left them to their speculation.

A STRUGGLE FOR BUNKS
ARMED ONLY WITH A CHOCOLATE BAR

We returned back to the hotel at about 4.00 o'clock to gather our limp assortment of greying underwear from the radiators into knapsacks already straining to straddle our new pink sink wardrobes. Our ferry left at 10.00 o'clock that night and the prospect of a trip across the yellow sea on a slow boat to China tickled our romantic fancies. We sat by the air brick in our hotel room and breathed in carbon monoxide while we deliberated excitedly over our itinerary for the next few days until the landlady came and told us to leave. We suspected it was not the impunity with which we swallowed lethal fumes or the fact that we'd unblocked the air-brick but the straggled-looking tribe of Kiwi backpackers that glimpsed dolefully over her shoulder that prompted our eviction. We feared for the safety of those six aerobic males in that tiny airless room.

Four hours later, we found ourselves boarding the Sunday night ferry to Hong Kong. Laura clutched a pathetic bundle of toilet roll (illicitly purloined from our hotel room) to her chest and I a selection pack of out-of-date western chocolate bars. These were inadequate tools given the fact that the ship was experiencing a total loss of power (not a good omen, I reluctantly concurred as a crunchie bar starting dripping down my leg). We reluctantly admitted that a flashlight or

Swiss-army -knife may have lent us more authority in the rush for bunks that ensued.

We followed a couple of "regulars" through a seedy back passage that seemed to run through the very bowels of the ship, depositing us like hamsters tumbling out of a rotastack chute onto a large empty deck. Our unwitting guides then scurried along another metal-floored walkway emerging with a triumphant saunter just outside the first of a series of dormitories. The throng advanced at us through the darkness with flashlights poised and a maniacal gleam in their eyes. It was like something from the Thriller video. We daren't risk a tussle (a limp mars bar wielded little power in these desperate times) so we dashed into the nearest dorm that had the character for "female" (wrongfully interpreted during the earlier part of our trip as *duck* - we did wonder why ducks and men got toilets while women peed in the street) on its door. Through the darkness we groped, feeling the warm hessian roughness of the bedding and an occasional hairy leg, until we came to two bunks tucked right away in the corner of the cabin. There we defiantly flung our bags, laid the remainder of our underwear out to dry, and strategically opened our Chinese phrase books so people would know we were friendly.

Now it was time to head onto the deck, something that I had been looking forward to for about 13 months, since the idea to do this trip had first entered our heads. Leaving behind the pandemonium of flying luggage and flailing arms we climbed a narrow rung of steps in the darkness and found ourselves on deck. The sky opened before us, the deepest darkest black rimmed with orange where it melted into the symphony of lights that decorated Hong Kong at night. The waters were gentle and held the reflections in perfect, silent, stillness, from the vivid blues and greens of the electronics magnates' giant neon signs to the tiny glimmer of street lights outside harbourside cafes. The rumour of the engine's chokes and grumbles brought others onto the deck, and we all stood in silence and watched as Hong Kong receded into a furry orange blur on the horizon. The air that swilled over us, warm as sand-dunes, was tinged with salt and fish and spice and a hint of diesel from the engine. Tomorrow, after a long and dark and sweaty night, would bring us to China's door.

CHINA

DICKENS WOULD HAVE LIKED THIS PLACE...

I awoke early, anxious to avoid the inevitable queues and further deterioration of the three public toilets on the whole ship designated for women and ducks. With the sun filtering through the remnants of a thick yellow band of fog that had stolen the China sea, I stole on deck to watch the first fog-smudged views of China hone into view. A soup of mud and decaying birds and fish sludged wearily around the stern of the ship, lapping apathetically at the trailing ropes and muddying the Ship's smart lettering with its grimy fingerprints. The air too, seemed brown and the stench of fish and diesel fumes stole the air from the back of my throat. It must have been the yellow fumes, but the memory I preserved from that moment is painted in my mind in sepia tones on a yellowed piece of parchment, like an old map or a carefully kept photograph in some old museum album. Somehow the scene seemed more poignant for its poisoned seas and yellow mists. I half-expected junk ships swarming with swash-buckling pirates to emerge from the mists brandishing swords and gangways and riggings, their murderous cries curdling the orange crowds. I felt like a time traveller visiting a place that had grown old and faded, its seas sleeping now and its shoreline folded in the clouds. I stood quietly for a while, until the yellow turned to brown on the skyline and the first brooding cut-out of China's southern coast took shape in the clouds. A waft of acrid fumes from the shoreline washed over the boat stinging my eyes. Then half the population of the boat erupted from the stairwells with a cheer, skittering onto the deck in a loud burbling mass like the outpourings of a storm drain in summer.

As the shoreline loomed into view, that Victorian artist painted in a fronting of sandy coloured factory buildings with broken windows and boarded up doors, and a row of seedy lime green and orange houses peppered between the old warehouses. Then the boat pulled up into a long channel and the waterfront slunk out of sight. After an interminable customs experience during which I nearly fainted from the heat and Laura experienced some obscure colonic rumblings, we tried to find a taxi. Thinking there was probably a predictable fare system in place, we leapt in the first taxi that came along. The driver did seem to smile at us in a rather sinister way as he set off along a peculiarly deserted road but we attributed it to local charm and a natural reserve with foreigners. Half an hour later and we still hadn't arrived in Canton, which we knew we had seen from the ferry laid out cleanly along the harbourside. Canton? Canton? we persisted, smiling and being very convivial. He smiled in the manner of a man enjoying a fat and delicious joke. "STOP" we screeched finally, and he pulled to a stop. "C-A-N-T-O-N", we pleaded, drawing out the Chinese characters and pointing back from whence we'd come. "Eh, Canton", he concurred with a definite twinkle dancing in his eyes. He turned around, and beneath the chunting of the engine we could hear the gurgling throbs of a low chuckle simmering in the back of his throat. When we finally got back to downtown Canton and unloaded our bags he charged us nearly ten American dollars. That afternoon we'd walk to the ferry in just seventeen minutes.

We now found ourselves standing, frothy lunged from the chemical fumes and wobbly from the traffic, outside what must be one of the grimmest places on Earth. Canton Railway Station. It reminded me of a book I'd read in Sunday School about Heaven and Hell. In this book God took the colour from the world and put it all in heaven. Hell was left grey and airless, and the people lived in a building that looked like an old Workhouse, lining up in endless shuffling rows to exhort spoonfuls of gruel from the grey-faced custodian of Hades while all around hammered the inhuman cries and clanging of men working the galleys. Mewling children fluttered on the fringes of huge crowds of faceless faces waiting despondently for a passage out of the grime and heat. Despite the evident influence of Dickens, the Reverend Chow must at least once have visited Canton Railway station.

My first thought was that grey, not red, should be the colour associated with communism. Faces, clothes, buildings, skies, the world was all daubed with the colour of concrete. We stuck ourselves onto the back of the shortest of the queues anticipating a 2-3 hour wait for our tickets. That counter closed for no apparent reason and we trailed a hundred feet back towards the harbour to join the end of another line. It was only when we checked the guidebook that we remembered how "aliens" in China enjoy the privileges of a two tier hospitality system - for a mildly inflated price we could bask in the air-conditioned comfort of the China Travel Service office and wallow in the palpable hostility exuded by the stern-faced sales attendants. It seemed a fair enough system to me, the privilege of visiting a country with such a learned and extravagant history was compensation enough for any fare hike. We copied down the Chinese characters for "Shanghai" and tried to look appealing. "Please, please get us out of here" was not in our Cantonese phrasebook but we pantomimed our way through a humiliating charade of our most urgent expressions. A dapper official gave us a key with the duck sign on it and gesticulated with a scowl in the direction of the washroom. We shook our heads and gestured with wilder urgency. At last he seemed to understand and began scribbling with equal urgency in his little notebook. The date, next to a drawing of a three wheeled train driven by what appeared to be a large chicken, was four days away. I scribbled it out and wrote tomorrow's date down with a large exclamation mark and my most hopeful smile. He countered with what I assumed from his firmly set and strangely dimpled chin was his best offer. But it was not soon enough. The throat eroding acid that seemed to blow in from the Sino-Chem chemical facility with each flock of dingy looking seagulls started another airborne invasion of our vital respiratory passages and between coughs we scribbled out all trace of the train and drew a picture of an aeroplane followed by three more exclamation marks. He scribbled down a sum in yuan that even with our rudimentary understanding of the currency system, seemed more than outrageous. With a dwindling sense of hope at ever getting out of the railway station, we handed over our special alien currency and purchased two train tickets out of Canton. Two days, four hours and two minutes to go.

HORRORS JUST AROUND THE CORNER...

Resigned to spending two more nights in Canton, we set off to find somewhere to stay. All the youth-hostels were fully booked, the most notorious of which being closed indefinitely for renovation and relocated to a small Presbyterian church which on closer inspection was found to be carefully boarded up. Eventually, sick of trailing our rucksacks and small collection of Japanese iron-ware around Canton, we agreed to take a small room in a tiny hotel above what seemed to be an abattoir. Air-conditioning was not an option at this place. It was not even a dim possibility. Fortunately there appeared to be a bed and something resembling a tap stuck about six feet up the wall. A small pair of fold-away steps covered the last remaining two square feet of floor space, presumably to help short people like me reach the tap. We hid our rucksacks under the bed, and left to explore the rest of Canton, but not before setting a careful booby-trap involving a small pottery horse and half a ton of Nambu iron-ware.

We headed off onto Shamian island into a world of decaying colonial houses the colour of turmeric and rosewater with fat balconies rimmed by ornate iron railings and crumbling gardens laid out with overgrown stepping stones and collapsing arbours overhanging dried-out ponds. This area became a French and British concession after China's defeat in the Opium Wars and was a one time a bustling trading and residential community. Now it resounded with the hollow clang of a Coca-Cola can clattering along the gutters and the cries of little children skittering through the crumbling gardens.

Behind this, off the island, the wide boulevards opened into a catacomb of tiny backstreets where all the stuff of our worst nightmares came to life. Whatever we'd seen in Hong Kong paled into humane insignificance next to this. Kittens and puppies mewled helplessly, tied in bundles by their tails to bloody racks that swung back and forth like the swing of the executioner's blade. It was impossible to process all the things we were seeing, the beggars that sprang from under market-stalls and garbage-rimmed alleyways to tug at our clothes, stalls selling monkeys trussed up like turkeys ready-made-up for the ritual head-splitting ceremony favoured for fashionable society occasions, bodies sleeping along the gutters, clothes sodden and smeared with the pulp that washed through the drains, unmentionable things reflected in stainless steel table-top chopping boards under spits loaded with snakes and toads and giant green salamanders.

We had heard on the ferry of a man who asked to buy a kitten so he could set it free in the streets. He chose his kitten with great care, the one that looked strongest, most likely to survive. When he pointed to a bright-faced grey tabby with rolling eyes the market-stall owner whipped it down by its tail, flung it head down on the steel slab and sliced straight through its neck. We had no doubt now that the story would have been true. Just as I reflected on this, we saw a lady fling a baby on its back on the same metal slab that the kittens felt cold under their noses before the knife came down. We winced in disbelief, paralysed momentarily as she reached for a knife. With open mouths we watched her draw the knife alongside its belly. A sigh of relief. She'd sewn its nappy together with cotton and was cutting her young son free. Our hearts did a somersault. Death and life danced hand-in-hand through the streets while Laura and I teetered delicately through the beggars, rubbish, sleeping bodies and dismembered animals like Victorian women with sickly constitutions.

The markets opened into a wider, squarer area where the endless bleeping of a million hand-held video games finally drowned-out the interminable bleating of Canton's billion sparrows. Every person here held a portable play-station in one hand and a wallet of bulging notes in the other. Videogames stacked high in teetering cardboard columns lined the street. Among the high tech carnage were strewn boxes of dubious cinematic content branded explicit, highly explicit and ultra explicit for easy selection. Apparently home-grown reproductions of famous western epics, the salesmen boasted proudly of the talents of local rising stars. Fat wads of notes flicked from the hands of men in suits to sharp traders in mean shirts and shades that were out of place on this cloudy day.

The roads here were owned by kamikaze madmen who carried their entire families on the back of prehistoric motorcycles, men weaving bikes with buckled wheels between potholes, saddlebags bulging with piglets and chickens and bags of yellow spice, and a man on a three-wheeled motorcycle with a full-sized pig riding in his sidecar. It was as if someone had thrown all the condemned cars and bikes and motorcycles into one big paper bag and was shaking them all around. The noise was interminable. Merchants bellowing , death-trap motor cycle engines roaring, bicycle bells ringing, brakes squealing, children bawling. Among all this, only the animals seemed to be silent.

ALL YOU REALLY NEED
IS A LOOSE PAIR OF MASSETER MUSCLES...

Our first night in Canton would later be remembered as the Ordeal of a Hundred Nightmares. Already forced to enjoy an unnatural intimacy by the fact that one of our beds inconveniently housed a cockroach nest in its mattress, we were then condemned to a night of sleepless anguish by the endless machinations of a devious and curiously persistent family of rats. Scared to face the descent to our basement toilet alone, we teetered together down the stairs in the middle of the night and took turns keeping a watchful guard on the abattoir doors. Returning safely to our room, we were sure we heard a faint squeak and a small rustling sound emanating from the general direction of our bed. Closer scrutiny revealed a neat pile of pygmy currants and a faint yellow dribble at the side of Laura's pillow. Laura's alarm seemed genuine so I could only conclude that a third, whiskered party had been the bestower of these fetid little offerings. Laura whipped the light on in a frenzy of general squeaking and proceeded to wake me up at regular intervals throughout the night to ask whether it was my snoring or the maniacal rantings of an asthmatic rat that she heard. It was a long long night.

Already Canton had outstayed its welcome in our trip. One day, four hours and twelve minutes till the moment of disembarkation. The next morning, awake early and feeling the need for air in our lungs, we decided to make a trip to the romantically named Lotus Mountain, forty-six miles south of Canton. The whimsically Enid Blyton-esque name conjured up graceful images of swaying concubines and elegant courtyards a-fluttering with bobbing jasmine blossoms and the dulcet music of a hundred bejewelled maidens. How wrong a name could be.

Two option had we, outlined the man who ran the abattoir, two option. We could take bus, or we could take boat. Each option was carefully delivered with all the pomp and solemnity of a funeral oration. The bus, he speculated wordlessly over a period of several minutes, might be quicker, but then, his cheeks scrunched up and his eyes rolled and he ruminated for another minute or so (marked only by the passing of a succession of impressive facial grimaces) on the idea that the boat might in fact be quicker. Fearful of ever making our escape from Canton, we thanked him profusely and sped away to find the harbour.

The boat left at 8.45 and we were the very last people to be squeezed on board. I ended up wedged next to a curiously small-headed man with an unfeasibly large paint brush who used his astonishingly mobile face to win favours with small children. Having wooed the child he would then exhort large amounts of money from the embarrassed parents for a very mediocre portrait of their little darling that they had not commissioned and could never hang for fear their child would grow up to hate them. Requiring no more skill that a peculiarly loose pair of masseter muscles and a devious wit the man was evidently onto a good thing. The spirit of free enterprise, we had heard, was at its most fervent and its most corrupt among the people of Canton, being so close to their avaricious cousins over the water and 2600 miles away from the entrepreneurial austerity practiced in Beijing. We had been astonished to see women with smart western perms, Sony Walkmans, Levi jeans and satellite dishes the size of small outhouses adorning the roofs of some houses. Indeed, the proprietor of one cafe boasted confidentially that he could get all the latest shows from Hong Kong, including (and this seemed to be a particular advantage for some reason) all the game shows. Twenty years ago exposure to such ruinous influences would have been considered highly detrimental to the moral cohesiveness of this incredible nation but now, as one young man in Levi's enunciated over a carcinogenic fizzy pop, it was all about money.

The deck of the boat was peppered with mah jong tables, a game I had yet to understand, and a swarm of disinterested looking vendors touting trays of soft drinks. China seemed to be obsessed with the miraculous process of carbonation. A young man in China was more likely to don a flowery smock and invite friends over for a baking party than he was to drink a glass of still orange juice. Bubbles were masculine, hip, happening and undeniably sexy. On every street corner a snappy dresser in shades would proffer bottles of Coca-Cola from a rusty wheelbarrow to men just dying to be cool. The really hip guys had a coke in one hand, a Godzilla video game in the other and an unfeasibly tight pair of trousers in between.

Without being picky, the term "mountain" was misleading. I had seen termite mounds all but desecrated by an unforeseen anteater attack that were taller than the Lotus Mountain. Furthermore, it was less of a mountain than a kind of hole really. A big craggy hole hacked out of the ground by a team of men, to be precise. Hard as the Chinese government had tried to dress up this giant quarry site with whimsical fake-pagoda accessories, the overall effect remained a large crater with lots of plastic Chinese buildings glued to its slopes. Actually the overall impression was of some kind of giant rock garden and was pleasing enough with its views of the Pearl River and the dense vegetation crowding down over the slopes, had each of its visitors not personally undertaken to dump at least half a hundredweight of non-degradable household waste in each of the cutsey little ponds. Plastic bottles, boxes filled with plastic margarine cartons, tarpaulin sheets, dirty laundry, fizzy drinks cans, empty beer bottles, ice trays, it was like some kind of ornamental recycling site. I had heard that following the irreversible purges of the twenty-year long Cultural Revolution, when the long traditions of Chinese culture and history were systematically eradicated and many material and spiritual connections to the old ways severed, that a movement towards preserving what cultural treasures survived was taking shape. Looking around me now, it seemed hard to believe.

YOU'D THINK THAT WOULD BE TRICKY IN A LEATHER BODY-STOCKING!

Surprisingly many happy hours had passed and we greeted the prospect of our return to Canton and our dismal sleeping arrangements with something less than enthusiasm but slightly more than absolute dread. This was the most positive we had felt all day so we embarked on a small ditty from Laura's native land of Manchester. As ever, approximately seven hundred grown-ups and children's stopped whatever they were doing to follow our every move. We had started to find it unnerving, this unflinching unselfconscious gaping that bore right into our every thought and action. We couldn't work out if it was a friendly or a hostile or a just plain curious kind of stare.

Later that night we found ourselves in Canton's cultural park surrounded by a hundred Chinese couples waltzing stiff-backed and stern-faced in impeccable rhythm and absolute silence between the trees that lined the roller-skating rink. Each couple seemed entranced in its own graceful dance as if concentrating on some special, intimate symphony that sang secret directions to their slippered feet and drew their eyes to a warm and distant light behind the trees. In graceless contrast, fizzy-pop drinking men on skates strutted some funky skid moves in their unfeasibly tight trousers and conscientiously avoided the gaze of the girls that fluttered, fizzy-pop in hand, around the side of the rink.

Suddenly from behind us we heard the throbbing of a small jet engine and the ear-jarring burp of the what must have been the world's loudest car horn. Startled beyond belief and fearful of finding ourselves mown down by a small commercial airliner we ducked and threw our backpacks to the ground. To our embarrassment the rest of the world went on dancing, skating and chewing around us. Turning round we saw that we had our backs to a large matchbox style motorcycle-ramp at the top of which a man in a flying helmet and what appeared to be a leather body-stocking straddled the back of an enormous motorcycle. Before our astonished eyes he took off with an ear-shattering roar, hurtling towards certain death up a ramp that rose vertically into the night sky. He flew off the top of it and fell in agonising slow-motion back to Earth in an incredible 360 degree mid-air flip that brought him gently down over fifteen rubber tires and a fat man breathing fire to a dignified stop next to the ice-cream stall. All around us, people watched the man get off his bike and claim his hero's can of Coca-Cola with disinterested, even bored, expressions. They looked at him as if he were an ordinary little man buying his groceries in a perfectly ordinary supermarket in a perfectly ordinary little town where nothing extraordinary ever happens. It seemed strangely ironic that our every movement magnetically attracted hordes of curious onlookers yet this mighty display of Evil-Kinevil style madness generated not one ripple of excitement.

I'LL BRUSH THIS BABY DOWN:
SHE'LL BE AS GOOD AS NEW

It was at ten o'clock the next day that the train eventually left Canton. As we settled down on our unyielding wooden seats for the eighteen hour journey I stifled a token pang of nostalgia for Canton and turned my thoughts forward to Shanghai.

An hour into our journey I began to imagine weevils equipped with supercarbon drilling heads boring into my bottom.. The family of eight we were sitting with had cracked open five screw-top jam jars of cold green tea and were busy slurping away as we drew into the second hour of our trip. The train hammered through a hundred tiny towns and villages, where dismal parades of leafless, ash-dusted trees peered at us through a yellow fog. Neolithic monuments along the trackside saluted China's industrial achievements, chunky communist schoolgirls in pigtails and dungarees and hillbilly shirts leaping for joy under the shadow of black chimneys and gleaming chemical installations. There was a famous-five style cuteness to some of the posters, all beaming smiles and lashings of Maoist thought and all be home in time for tea and a healthy slice of revolutionary pie. The reality, we vaguely knew, had been harsh, but the images were winsome with their comradely backslaps and honest toil and at one with the earth-ish-ness. It was astonishing to me that a country with a documented history and culture spanning six thousand years could in the course of one century experience a philosophical and administrative and industrial shake-up that would force China's traditions underground, give rein to its tyrants and bring horror to its millions of citizens.

When we screeched to our first stop the older man jumped out and came back into the compartment with ten milk-coloured ice-lollies. There were dubious black crusty bits glued between the yellowing wrapper and the congealed ice and I knew what was about to happen. With a sinking heart, an incredible surge of gratitude, and all the health precautions I'd ever read ringing in my ears, I gingerly accepted the rancid lolly. It smelt of warm horses and something the size and texture of a small satsuma welled in my throat. The Li family studied us with the greatest interest as we delicately nibbled and sucked, Laura retching every now and then as she fished a dead fly from between her teeth. Twenty minutes into the lolly and no sign of the stick, I was forced to make a break for it. Waiting for a jolt that could legitimately unseat me, I threw my lolly into the lap of old Mr Li, where it wobbled precariously for a few minutes before tipping slowly onto the floor. I moved my face through the contortions of disappointment and wiped a small bug from my upper lip. Never fear, said Mr Li with a reassuring nod. Blowing away a couple of tenacious cigarette butts and pausing to wipe the stick on his jacket cuff, he picked up my lolly with a gentle smile. Laura gave me a particularly annoying smirk as she tossed her stick into the garbage. I suddenly had a sense of how precious luxuries like this must be and felt miserable about my ingratitude. I finished the lolly in the end, and paid for it on and off for the next few days, but I remembered the generosity of the Li family with pins beneath my nails and a cringe at my miserable rich-kid ness.

The Li family got off at the next station and three elderly men got onto the train. Thankful at the extra space, we welcomed them into our compartment. I busied down to writing a postcard to a young man called Seki I'd left behind in my Japanese village, trying to ignore the mounting crescendo of hawks and spits that were hailing down around our feet. With an extraordinary absence of self-consciousness these three men delivered fleshy little flem bullets into the cosmos with irritating regularity. It was an appalling tune that somehow stuck in my head as well as on my trouser leg and sole of my boot. I tried to suppress the involuntary little flinches that sparked through me everytime they ejaculated a small chunk of lung tissue. Apart from the obvious threat of disease, there was no reason except the unshakeable weight of social conditioning for us to be so repulsed by this. It was the same in Japan, the unrestrained burping and slurping and belching that screamed the politest of compliments to the cook, the hawking and spitting of nicotine-yellow mucus, the unrestrained testicular scratching. Mr O-yama in my office retaliated (when I delicately raised the subject) that the European habit of blowing one's nose and wedging the snot-encrusted rag back up one's sleeve was disgusting. The Japanese practice of complete and irreversible evacuation was healthier, he promised, alluding in sinister tones to Freud. His point was lost on me.

CHIANG KAI-SHEK HAD A VERY BALD HEAD...

One of the men, an unusually tall man with a fierce looking cane, was studying my postcard with the utmost concentration. Suddenly I was sure I 'd heard him say "Kon'nichi-wa". I looked over at him but he was looking with equal intent out of the window. Hmmm. I got back to writing my card. "Dozo". This time I definitely heard it. I looked at him accusingly but again he was looking away. "Nihongo ga hanasemasu ka?", I ventured, expecting him to bolt. "Hai, sukoshi wakarimasu" he answered warily, watching me out of the corner of his eye. Incredible. Here, in the middle of China, was a man speaking Japanese.

His name was Mr Song and it was many years since he'd spoken Japanese. For the longest time it had been forbidden to speak to foreigners or speak a foreign tongue in communist China. He explained how his father had joined the Koumingtang in its earliest days of the twentieth century when it was a political movement directed by Dr Sun Yatsen. I'd visited Hawaii several years before and on the spindly road that circumnavigated Maui's southern coast come across The Sun Yatsen Memorial Garden where two doleful looking stone lions and a round shouldered statue of a man in a raincoat stalked a small public park. There was no notice explaining who the round-shouldered man was or why he should be standing here under Maui's pregnant rain clouds in his raincoat. Sun Yatsen was a doctor from Canton who is credited with bringing together a number of anti-imperial revolutionary factions and launching lots of ill-fated anti-government coups which aborted at the last moment giving Sun the chance to holiday in Hawaii while things simmered down. (Like the Church, revolution has always been a cheap travel ticket).

Eventually the persistence of Sun's Alliance brought about the beginning of the end of the Qing dynasty in 1912, in the South of

China at least, though the ways of the ruling warlords held steady in the North. The Kuomintang, Sun's "alliance", held the reins of government now. It was the sorry but inevitable termination of an empire that had been disintegrating steadily over the previous fifty years under the domineering government of the Emperor Dowager Wu Cixi, a lady always pictured with seven inch fingernails and some kind of log contraption in her hair, both of which much surely have hindered the machinery of effective government. Convinced that modernisation might bring contact with Western hairdressers she had buckled down China's hatches and presided like a moody hen over the thrones of her son and grandson while revolt festered outside like some kind of big, inconvenient boil. At least we think that's what Mr Song alluded to. Impressively, despite the blazing sores of anti-Manchu hysteria that erupted from time to time, she kept her throne until her death in 1908 (her fingernails continued to grow for the next seven years). China was now in the care of her two year old grandson Pu Yi, The Last Emperor. His title gives the game away. Doomed from the start, he clung to a tissue paper existence with a staff of nursemaids and eunuchs until Sun's men came politely knocking and exiled him to China's brutal north-east frontier.

Meanwhile, Marxist thought had started to inseminate the minds of the bored and rankled. The formation in 1921 of The Chinese Communist Party brought this Century's big political players into one big communist casino. Under pressure from their big Russian brother, the Communists hesitantly joined forces with the faction-ridden Kuomintang the next year. A risky gambit while Sun was alive, it was a suicidal one after his death in 1925 when the Kuomingtang fell under the rule of ultra-paranoid militarist Chang Kai Shek who in the spirit of the military fundamentally opposed social reform and wanted to recreate a society ruled by an effete elite and supported by a hard-line military dictatorship. Oh yes, with himself as head. He was a very bald man, gestured Mr Song, wiping his hand over the top of his head, and wore false teeth from a very early age.

Given the Communists' commitment to global social reform and Chiang Kai Shek's outright abhorrence of poor people, the union was for ever ill-fated. Meanwhile Mao proselytised in the country and was dismissed as an eccentric yokel with a penchant for horsehair. The faction-infected Kuomintang was busy planning its Northern Expedition to oust those troublesome warlords once and for all, along the road from Canton to Shanghai, where we ourselves were now headed. In Shanghai communist workers and foreign sympathisers were set to bring the city to a standstill while Chiang ousted the warlords. Treachery, though, was in Chiang's mind. He armed hundreds of Shanghai's mobsters and dressed them in Kuomintang fatigues before unleashing them on the worker's militia. Hundreds, if not thousands of workers were killed. Mr Song's father was there, right behind Chiang Kai Shek and he saw it all. Like all the young men who followed Chiang Kai Shek, he hadn't known what was going to happen. The reins of government passed to Chiang Kai Shek and his military backers and the Communists walked away, for now. It was a black black day in China's history.

SHANGHAI: THE VILEST PLACE ON EARTH??

So this was the Shanghai to which we were now headed, the scene of one of China's greatest acts of treachery against China this century. Like any graduate of the 1980's with their endless, appalling karate movies, Shanghai was inextricably interwoven in my imagination with triads and opium smoking colonials and extravagant, reckless, stupid women with names like Georgie and Ginger. In the Shanghai I imagined, people languished in the smoky half-light of cocktail bars or in opium dens the colour of claret wine. In dazzling ballrooms dapper Chinese men with English names like Harry and Stephen would dance the latest western steps in stiffly creased Saville Row suits under chandeliers that filled the sky with stars. It was an elegant, lightless life I pictured, thin as tissue-paper, everything taking place in pouted half-whispers through plumes of cigarette smoke as if the bums and villains and beggars and adventurers who paced the streets outside might burst through the doors like some hideous musical finale and bring this tinsel-town show to an end.

Just like a Japanese history book, my entire knowledge of Shanghai stopped in the 1930's. Parasitically settled by the French, the English, the Italians, the Americans and the Japanese, the International Settlement in the 1930's boasted the largest number of motor vehicles, the most spacious cinemas and the tallest buildings of anywhere in Asia. The World's largest banking houses lined the Bund, the riverfront world of commerce and trading that flanked China's Pacific Coast. The Yangtse and Huangpu rivers were patrolled with ships scouted by Japanese blue-jackets, British Tommies, Italian, French and American marines. It was a home from home, arrogantly immune from Chinese law and openly contemptuous of Chinese culture. The British controlled the International Concession's police force, colluding handsomely with Chiang's forces and his underworld colleagues in suppressing labour unrest among the Chinese workers. But outside this "scrupulous" and paranoid community with its starched linens and high teas, double standards, atrocious social conditions and immense injustices perpetrated in the name of industrialisation were a fact of daily life. It was no secret that young children were indentured into bonded labour in Shanghai's million silkshops working twenty-hour days by the light of a spindly candle. It was no secret that child prostitution was "indulged" in the dimly lit brothels that flanked the ports. It is strange how one can, without a hint of irony, set standards for the people of one's own country and yet care so little for the fate of another country's men, women, and children. It's as if we don't see them as people at all.

Ultimately, of course, it was the Japanese who would come to control Shanghai, for ten years at least. By 1930, there were thousands of Japanese troops on China's North-East, Manchurian border. Chiang dismissed the imminent threat of a Japanese invasion as a trifling inconvenience and remained paranoically dedicated to his life-long goal of eradicating the communists, whose Oscar Wilde caps and androgynous womenfolk made him uncomfortable. It eventually took a nocturnal kidnapping escapade in which Chiang was ingloriously held captive by his own men and forced to hide behind a rock in his night-shirt while the rebels used his false teeth in a succession of disappointing practical jokes to make him see sense. Agreeing reluctantly to a temporary anti-Japanese truce with the Communists Chiang half-heartedly menaced the Japanese from afar while plotting extermination raids against the real communist menace.

Chiang was a man whose ego needed to be stroked History remembers him as an arbitrary, intractable bully with a habit of resigning every now in a petulant temper just to make the country come grovelling to him on its rudderless knees. While he plotted his raids and disappeared for a sulk in the country, the Japanese slowly took over most of Eastern China. It was only in 1941, when the Japanese bombed Pearl Harbour and America stepped into the war, that the Japanese were finally ousted from China.

Mr Song had started off in the Kuomintang, fighting for Chiang just like his father had done. But after the Shanghai massacre he defected, joining the Communists in 1945 along with millions of other young men who broke from the Kuomintang ranks. By the next year the communists had armed most of their men with Sherman tanks confiscated from the Kuomintang and Chiang was sent skittering with the Country's entire bullion reserves to Taiwan, where only the Americans continued to recognise him as China's undisputed leader. That, explained Mr Song, was the official start of Communist China.

The train slowed down as it pulled into a small town; Mr Song and his companions got ready to disembark. They lived in Nanjing but were breaking their journey here for a few days to visit family. In perfect copperplate handwriting he wrote down his address and bid us come visit him when he got back to Nanjing and we promised that we would.

IS THAT REAL FILTER COFFEE?

We awoke the next morning drenched in sweat and scored by the pin-cushion pricks of a million blood-sucking bed-bugs. They left their signatures in welty Braille across our backs and legs. The apathetic trickle of the ceiling fan muddying the steamy air was soporific and we lay in a delirious dream-state while mosquitoes performed aerial acrobatics in our ears and the bed-bugs swarmed our bodies. I eventually rattled my brain awake and trudged down the corridor to the bathroom where the empty shower cubicle promised a soothing, balming morning rain . The term shower was a misnomer. Limp, dismal muddy drip would have been more appropriate. I shivered pathetically waiting for each "blip" sound so I could smear the cold brown blob over my body.

After a few minutes a heavy knocking came to my door. I replied in English that I wouldn't be a minute, thinking it must be another guest. The knocking continued and I answered again. After a minute the hammering stopped and I huffed an indignant sigh of relief. Then to my surprise, while studying the trickle of brown mud running off my toes, the face of an elderly Chinese woman materialised at the bottom of my shower cubicle door. I reached for my towel. She was gesticulating crossly with pointed fingers and generally making lots of noise. As I came out, she hurried into the cubicle dragging behind her a large basket stuffed with clothes. Hitching her long skirt into her waistband and dropping to her haunches she began to scrub her clothes in the greying trickle of my shower. I turned around to find at least five other older Chinese ladies with laundry baskets lining up to go into the shower.

We were staying in the Shanghai music conservatory, a colonial relic from Shanghai's international hey-day. It still housed students in the term-time but in the holidays it was possible to secure fairly clean and spacious rooms for a nominal housekeeping fee. We were intoxicated by the very idea of staying in such a grand-sounding place. For Laura, with all her classical inclinations and dubious fascination with eunuchs, this was one step down from kipping in Prokofiev's privy. She was quite uncontrollable with excitement. The rooms were reminiscent of a boarding school dormitory, un-inspirationally decorated with magnolia walls and a forgettable brown carpet. But the noise was other-worldly. Our night had been punctuated by the asthmatic wheezing of a junior trombonist, the champion belching of a tuba, the squeal of an abused violin, the slap and squeak of bats against our mosquito nets and finally at four o'clock this morning the metal-chewing growl of a concrete mixer being started up outside our window.

The streets were filled with the most calamitous dim as all things two legged, three legged, four legged and occasionally legless, as well as a whole circus parade of wheeled contraptions, clanged their way down the rickety roads. Lane discipline was apparently a concept yet to reach the East. We manoeuvred our way through the frothing bedlam to find some breakfast, having discovered that a small army of black beetles have buried their way into our sacred bread supply.

Before we had gone twenty feet, we were flagged down by a toothless old man in a padded jacket that must have functioned like a roasting bag in this excessive heat. He insisted that Mrs Thatcher had visited China at least fifteen times and recounted a story about a famous English prophet called Mr Water who seemed to have been turned into a chicken. We rifled frantically through our dictionaries but still could make no sense of it. Mrs Thatcher and Mao Tsetung, he proclaimed with an evangelical flourish were like brother and sister and the Americans were all cheats, liars and general scoundrels. I wondered what he said to the Americans. His English was excellent but by this time at least three thousand people had gathered around us. Prone to claustrophobia I immediately red-flagged this as a potentially toxic situation and began furtively scanning for emergency exit-routes. Our friend headed off with his bicycle to drink his tea.

We decided to take advantage of the fact that we were in the French Concession to visit the JingJiang Hotel, a colossal 15 story monument to the imported concession culture of the 1920's. It was like finding the Titanic alive and well and magically restored to all its Edwardian glory at the bottom of the ocean among the barnacles and algae. We wondered how such an extravagant monument to the capitalism of the foreign devils, had survived the anti-bourgeois purges of the cultural revolution, particularly given Shanghai's traditional role as custodian of dogmatic Maoism through the last fifty years.

Breakfast at the JingJiang Hotel was legendary and imported, eggs and bacon and toast and real marmalade, orange juice that had once been an orange and real Kona coffee that didn't leave a film of scum around your mouth when your cup was empty. We declined the speciality eggs which our waitress assured us could be cooked "rare". We nursed a warm glow of contentment in our bosoms as we munched on this nostalgic feast. After two years of dried fish, tofu, fermented soy beans and spring onions for breakfast, the sweetness of real marmalade erupted like a firework display on our tongues. The hotel itself was pretty much closed to non-residents but we embarked on a furtive reconnaissance mission after breakfast. Every time the elevator door opened we expected to be escorted back to the streets by a burly security official but as we rose higher and higher we started to develop a cocky sense of invincibility. We stopped flinching each time we saw waiters and waitresses, chambermaids and bellboys. Ironically, despite the terminal condition of our flip-flops, hair and personal hygiene, and that fact that we could not make in five years what it cost to spend one night here, our blotchy white faces seemed passport enough to this exclusive and fading world.

On the fourteenth floor we emptied out into an amazing hallway where a magnificent clock marked time against a background of intricately hand-painted peach blossoms. One of the chambermaids came bustling through with her duster and a veritable wagon of cleaning supplies. She understandably looked a little surprised to see us standing there. We tried to explain that we just wanted to look, we wouldn't touch anything; she took a key from her pocket and with a finger to her lips led us into a magnificent dining hall where the deepest rosewood chairs and tables waited stiff-backed and patient for the slap of an auspicious bottom, a mayor perhaps, or a bishop. The room was presided over by a fragile filigree chandelier that tipped silver stars onto the mirror-finish tables and melon yellow walls. Bamboo screens carved out secluded corners where gleaming brown leather armchairs skulked moodily; you could almost still make out a fine mist of cigarette smoke or the warm indentation of Saville-Row-suited bottom on the leather seat. It was as if Al Capone himself had just left the room.

ITS RAINING:
DON'T FORGET YOUR SHOWER-CAP!

The first clouds appeared as we came up behind The Bund, Shanghai's former Wall street, where unfeasible fortunes were made and spectacular crashes lamented in the heyday of the early twentieth century. It was a fragile, paper-thin world where destinies were spun overnight from green dollar bills and lives tipped upside-down at the flick of an abacus bead. I had read many books alluding to this clandestine world and was excited to be in a place that was pivotal to world history in so many unrecognised little ways. The Bund's imported hotchpotch architecture, grand and austere and stately, was flanked by huge strips of pavement had been torn up as part of a "landscape" renovation project and a spidery mesh of bamboo and string scaled most of the more prominent buildings. Still there was a sense of unimaginable past riches and a hint of the thrill that those early traders must have felt as they glided into the harbour. I thought of Dick Whittington approaching London and wondered what disappointments waited in the sidestreets for those early newcomers. It must have been hard to find lodgings, rents would have been high, and gangs would have controlled most of the streets, from the beggars to the men who owned the big hotels. Chiang Kai Shek himself had been among the companions of a buck-toothed underworld leader who had helped Chiang organise the 1931 volte-farce that would kill thousands of Shanghai workers and give him leadership of the Kuomintang. Yes, there was definitely something utterly sinister, yet entrancing about this city. Passionate, romantic, sophisticated. The Panama hat and opium glamour of those 1930's movie-set straggled on in the dimly lit smoking bars with their red and green disco lights.

Except that luxurious silk stockings had been tragically superseded by The Pop-Soc in a variety of American tan hues and three fetching styles - the ankle look, the shin and the full knee-length queen of a pop-soc in chocolate brown only. Some had patterns, some were plain. Women mostly, but some men, with their unnaturally brown feet and white strappy sandals, paraded their imports with a curious lack of self-consciousness. That afternoon we found ourselves in Pop-Soc City, otherwise known as the No.1 Department Store, where the latest fashions and consumables could be procured - as long as you wanted pop socs (in a range of fetching faecal hues), fizzy pop (including an import from India called Thumbs Up) or hand-held computer games. The windows were awry with curiously large-headed mannequins with unfeasible bosoms and strangely amorphous mouldings in the genital region. Everything sort of smudged together making the fine distinction between men and women (both had breasts) tricky. However, the female mutant seemed to be favouring dark brown pop socs, the male variant a more fetching shade of light tan. Those mannequins who were dressed wore selected terylene fashions in that season's unusual citrus tones. Vivid lemon, putrefying lime green and a dubious tangerine colour that reminded me of sherbet. The newest item on the block, fresh from the capitalist catwalk, was the shower cap. Not the sleek, rubberised models favoured by Speedo and all self-respecting aquarians but the flower-decked, nylon studded, fruity creation favoured by 1950's belles in Elvis movies. When, on leaving the store, it started to rain, we were astonished to see 35 grown women don shower caps abloom with plastic roses, lilies and small ornamental cherries. Those who didn't have a shower cap produced a strange kind of baseball cap with a perspex umbrella attachment stuck on top of it. I felt quite the frump in my raincoat.

It was something that I found amazing for all the time we were in China. Despite the so-called freedom we enjoy as Brits and Germans and Japanese, we were all tied up in behavioural straight-jackets that lent an often unconscious self-consciousness to our movements, our actions, our mannerisms, our appearance. Where here, people did (at least what seemed to us to be) the most bizarre things with the least regard for the wider approval or attention of those around them. It was an interesting slant on the word liberation.

GRUELLING GASTRONOMY!

We chose a restaurant called Yanzhon for our evening meal. The waitress apologetically put us together with another couple. We didn't appreciate the true extent of her apology until we saw the couple. The man was completely intoxicated, dribbling profusely and spitting all over the table. He kept beckoning over the waitresses with a conspiratorial air and stuffing money into their pockets, which his wife, with an embarrassed smile, kept getting up to retrieve. Every few minutes he'd let forth a violent belch, retch heavily from the stomach and appear ready to burst forth with noodles and carrots but always at the last moment regain control and with a smug burp sink back into his chair. Then along came a very aggressive waitress who told us to pick up our feet before blasting the floor under our feet with enough industrial roach killer (administered through something resembling a nuclear warhead) to kill a small island nation. The drunken man promptly fell off his chair into the foamy roach-killing slime and added his own personal contribution to SinoChem's patented life-extinguishing formula. His lady-friend left him there splashing impotently in the corrosive slush while helping herself to the remains of his chicken dinner.

On offer were such delicacies as duck webs and fish head soup, five assorted periwinkles in chicken blood, sautéed frogs with braised chicken feet and other X-rated family favourites. China's rich language and love of metaphor has suffused its varied mistreatments of animals with a whimsical poeticism. The dish of three squeaks for example, is a delicacy featuring live rat embryos. The point, it is said, being that the first squeak is heard when the chopsticks touches the animal, the second when it hits the soy sauce and the third..... Or the dance of a thousand purple petals. A dog is tied at each foot to a square wooden frame and then skinned while still breathing. Released, it hobbles in great pain through the streets dropping "petals" of blood into the streets. When it finally collapses, exhausted, it is eaten. There is no accounting for taste. This restaurant featured the "pig face" speciality. The face of a live pig is coated with wax; then the wax is ripped off, the skin of the pig's face comes off too. Used in an exciting variety of special dishes the face is apparently flavoursome and exotic. On neither count could we be induced to try it.

YES, OUR TOILETS ARE VERY PUBLIC

By three o'clock we both desperately needed to find a toilet. In the backstreets of a bustling bazaar we hunted down The Mandarin Gardens, thinking there would certainly be a toilet there. This was where the government, with touching disregard for irony, had created concrete and Styrofoam replicas of imperial buildings that it had destroyed during The Cultural Revolution. Impressive when viewed from the front, the monuments' glory dimmed when approached from the rear - a tangled ladder of iron bars and concrete posts yet to be hand-painted with authentic Ming Dynasty designs. And not a toilet in site. Disappointed, we ran back into the winding catacombs that swarmed over most of downtown Shanghai. On a precarious wooden stool an elderly man cut his toe-nails with a rusted pair of garden shears. Behind him queues of people lined up to have their hair cut with chopping knives in metal chairs that had arm and waist straps like the electric chairs we saw in movies. Above us terylene shirts and skin-pink perspex underwear in three chunky dimensions dried stiffly on washing lines alongside ducks and skinned animals in the sweltering midday sun. We ran through streets silted up with rotten fruit in frantic search of a toilet, but saw nothing that looked at all promising except a bucket full of hair clippings and a hollowed out cantaloupe.

It didn't help that people were washing in the muddy brown water that sprang from a gash in the paving slabs. All this water gurgling and splashing and bubbling - it was torture. Women dangling out of apartment windows above us slopped buckets of a dubious muddy brown water onto the streets like a scene from some Shakespearean soap-opera and we winced as our bladders contracted. Fat, toad-sized muddy-brown bombs hailed down around us splattering up our legs and arms. We hurried to the relative safety of an open park area. "Toilet?" I asked one man, with my usual euphemistic chain-flushing, hand-washing gesture and a look of sheer desperation in my eyes. He studied us both for a long time, looking us carefully up and down before answering with a hint of hesitation - - - "No-o". The next man we asked tried to sell us black-market tickets for "Gone with The Wind", the latest cinematic smash to hit the Chinese box offices. But the lady behind him pointed round the corner and we hurried on into a solid grey concrete building that seemed curiously deficient in the way of doors.

Greeted first by a completely naked lady washing her clothes in the cistern who asked us for an admission fee, I turned around to find an open sewer running through the centre of the room. Women squatted over this channel nose to bottom to nose to bottom. Reluctant to take my place in this lavatorial chorus line I realised that my alternatives were limited. I straddled the sewer in conspicuous slow-motion, fearful of losing my grip and tumbling into the slurping river. Immediately ten pairs of eyes turned to face me. Furthermore, a fundamental design flaw left us exposed in every sense to the scrutiny of the Chinese public walking past the door As is always the way, performance anxiety froze my aching bladder and one by one, each individual thigh muscle as I squatted under the scrutiny of twenty-five fascinated people. I wondered what they thought British shit might look like. Two minutes passed and still a frustrating lack of flow. There was no doubt that by this stage everyone had noticed my failure to perform. Hauling myself back up to standing, with as much dignity as possible, I walked carefully out of the door looking very much as if I'd just got off a horse. Public, in the toilet sense, had never had meant so literally.

THE JADE BUDDHA

The motorcycle policeman who first gave us directions to The Jade Buddha kept reappearing round every corner to hurry us on our way. No one ever seemed to notice him despite the throbbing phut-phut of his prehistoric motorcycle combination or the large sack of melons he carried in his side car. I wondered if he was really some kind of benevolent ghost with a mission to guide lost souls on their way and we'd later read that he'd been killed years earlier in a freak accident involving cantaloupes. Perhaps it was just that our pasty whiteness attracted so much attention that a melon bearing communist official went unnoticed.

The Buddha lived in a mango coloured temple where cheery-faced men in string vests smiled widely at the sight of our foreign exchange certificates and hurried us to meet their leader, a warm-faced man in resplendent robes carving some kind of face out of a watermelon with the ceremonial temple dagger. His attendants, in slightly less splendid robes, nodded profusely at us over gaping red watermelon slices that pointed up or pointed down, giving the monks sad melon mouths or happy melon mouths like the chorus line in some Punch and Judy show. The overall effect was of lots of toothless old men with some kind of highly contagious gum-disease.

Just at that serene moment, seven hundred or so Japanese tourists shuffled in in a tittering flurry of shoe-removing, back-bending obsequiousness, all bums and bare feet and flapping camera bags. They flashed briefly, each one of them, before magically relocating their own shoes among hundreds of identical lace-ups and rustling out again in one big twittering swarm. Laura and I were still grappling with our clumsy woollen laces as their coach pulled away. Only the smell of dettol and a fine mist of flaking fish bits remained.

The Buddha himself wore a Mona-Lisa like expression, serene on the surface but underneath enjoying a good laugh at the Japanese people too. Sculpted in solid jade, (though some say it is really alabaster) the statue was brought from Burma over 400 years ago. It was impossible to imagine quite how such a journey could have been undertaken, given his size and presumably weight. "Spiritual lightness" declared one of the monks, a melon pip wobbling precariously on his upper lip. I admired his reasoning but doubted he'd ever carried four tons of religiously enlightened jade on his shoulders.

Buddhism, China's principle religion, accepts the tenet of reincarnation, that we are rewarded or punished for our deeds in this life by rebirth as a meerkat or anteater or elephant in the next one. Personally I rather fancied coming back as some kind of whimsical woodland creature so I could cavort in mossy groves with my furry forest chums and spend my whole life digging up food. It seemed a health-conscious and environmentally low-impact lifestyle that offered inexhaustible prospects for forest frolics. I'd seen Wind in The Willows and quite fancied myself in a little green corduroy jacket. Surprisingly, however, the ultimate goal of Buddhism was not to be reborn as a squirrel (there was still a lot I had to learn) but to not come back at all, which seemed something of a cop-out. Apparently, the founder of Buddhism, an Indian man called Siddartha, had become so disillusioned with his privileged lifestyle that he renounced it all to become a wandering asthetic with a penchant for horsehair and an endless list of pilgrimages and penances in his daytimer. Buddhists find life on the whole a fairly depressing affair, lots of suffering and grief than man can, through enlightenment, escape, to reach nirvana. Desire is apparently the really corrosive force in society and the thing man must try and shake off if he is to be liberated at all from the mortal trappings of his this-world-liness.

But Buddhism is not the only stream of thought penetrating the greater Chinese consciousness. The Chinese religion, explained the Chief Monk, is animistic in the sense that it believes in the innate vital energy of rocks, trees, mud, rivers and springs, which helped us understand the cult of Chinese pop-idol worship a little better. People's ancestors, from the near and distant past, are also guaranteed to be worshipped as gods after their death, which is always nice. On top of that add a dash of Taoism, which combines with old animistic beliefs to teach people how to maintain harmony with the universe, and a splash of Confucianism, which takes care of the political and moral aspects of life, along with a big spoonful of Buddhism. No wonder we were confused.

The chief monk invited us to take a stroll around the walls of the temple, both inside and out, while he finished his melon. Apparently he'd just found a lovely juicy bit that would require a lot of sucking so we would have to be quiet and stop asking questions. At least we think that's what he said. On the periphery of one of the courtyards, but just inside the temple walls, a small stall had been set up selling temple souvenirs and "luck-predictions". With a pippy gurgle and an expansive hand gesture, the monk invited us to try our luck. I picked out a piece of paper that could have said "may your eldest daughter have ears like a donkey", but I nodded and looked delighted as if this was the news I had been always been waiting for. It was astonishing to see fortune-telling out there in the open, enjoying an almost symbiotic relationship with one of the world's most ancient religions. I wondered fleetingly if the Monk was on commission. He looked a little disappointed as he fingered his little strip of "fortune-paper" and I feared there would be tears before lunchtime. Later on our trip someone would say to us - "The Chinese are very flexible and like to keep their options open". Apparently a reference to the astuteness of Chinese financial planning, I could see what he meant!

As we left, the chief monk held out a slice of watermelon in one hand and a small collecting tin in the other, but not before asking us "Change Money?". We made a handsome contribution and purchased the most expensive piece of fruit known to modern Chinese history.

YOU CAN NEVER KNOW ENOUGH ABOUT THE HISTORY OF GERMAN TOILET CISTERNS...

Frustrated with our recurrent water retainment difficulties we set off in search of a universal sink plug, an object so obscure that even our best charadery proved an impotent tool in our laborious, sweaty, search. No one seemed to understand us. Ever hopeful, we followed the road along a creek, where huge blue boat houses stood on stilts in the water, listing gently in the scorching sun. Allegedly the hub of the old gambling and opium scene, now a bedraggled collection of sinking wooden boathouses moored up in the putrid creek like crayfish trapped in a shrinking pond and waiting for the summer rains. Around the creek Macdonalds and posh frock shops and designer boutiques had sprung up, bright new shiny flowers that would suck the remaining water from the pond.

From the other side of the road Laura spotted a dimly lit building with rows of wheelbarrows and dubious plumbing appendages strewn all around. With its smoky windows and dark, clattering interior we thought we had surely found a Chinese Home Depot. We set off with great enthusiasm (anticipating the under-appreciated satisfaction of a full sink) across the road to find ourselves peering not at a friendly aproned man with a hammer but at hundreds of tellers neatly stationed in tidy rows sealed off by yellow perspex screens whirring their fingers across abacus beads by green bankers lamps that sell these days in Walmart for a couple of dollars. We questioned a tall man in a suit about sink plugs but he hurried away in a flustered pickle. The wheezing of the ratchet on the ceiling fan was the only sound except the hurried clicking of a million tiny coloured beads and the rasping of dry fingers shuffling dirty notes. It was like entering some strange submarine cave where the light filtered in through a film of algae and seaweed and the only sound was the clicking of a million little crab legs scurrying over the seabed. This was the Shanghai bank.

Precarious bamboo scaffolding twined around the building latching onto window ledges and door frames. A nervous-looking man in green overalls cast a jittery eye to the heavens in between offering hard hats at random to the richer looking customers. We felt his appraiser's eyes swiftly survey our potential life-worth and deem us not worth saving. There was no plug for us here.

Then we mimed our problem to the Foreman of Works, who was wearing something resembling a shower cap. He shook his head and called us a taxi. We seemed to have experienced a communication block but it seemed rude to refuse the taxi so we leapt in and asked the driver to take us to a hardware store. He seemed a little surprised but the driver of an electric bus gave him directions and we set off with high expectations. About thirty minutes later, after one last asthmatic belch, the taxi broke down. Thankfully Shanghai's traffic system is an elaborate ruse to keep government officials in their air-conditioned cars all day without having to actually do any work, so the driver of the electric bus was still just inches away. (In total we had moved about six feet. The meter had been running for about thirty minutes).

The tram driver gave us an obliging push onto the pavement, where we incurred a small knock from another vehicle taking an unorthodox short-cut. The taxi driver dismissed us into the hazards of rush hour but not before requesting his payment. We paid because we couldn't stand to think how much it would cost to fix his car.

Sitting in the taxi for thirty minutes had given us a chance to study our map and read our guidebook. by the time we got out again half an hour later, in exactly the same place, we had staked out a hardware store not too far away. Laura lead the way, gung-ho through the bustling backstreets full of chickens and bicycles and popsocs. Three wrong turnings and a dodgy confrontation with a pig (that we wiggled out of only through our judicious deployment of a small bag of watermelon pips) later, we found a sanitary appliances store, wedged between ten fruit stores on the one side and fifteen on the other. One thing led to another and before we knew it a round-faced man in glasses was uncovering his collection of ceramic lavatory bowls and a rare German toilet cistern salvaged from the international concession. It took half and hour to extricate ourselves from the store, plugless and armed with two slices of watermelon and valuable new knowledge about the black-market trade in sanitary commodities. We never did get our plug.

SPANDEX AND SPARKLES...

We had dinner that night in a tiny backstreet restaurant that looked cosy through the red-tinted windows. While Laura ordered, I went to the washroom, where two women rinsed sanitary towels in the sink while they talked. I was quite taken aback, being used to the discrete technology that "liberates" us western girls from the troubles of menstruation, relegating it to a minor inconvenience much like a pimple or a broken nail that can be "fixed" by some magical off-the-shelf product. At first we'd been surprised at the apparent availability of such items. Tampax were advertised on billboards and in magazines, always showing androgynous women in Victorian swimming costumes playing light-heartedly with large beach balls under a blistering sun and looking all homely and "free". Or gymnastic women bending backwards over trapeze wires in little sparkly costumes. What we hadn't taken into account, despite the conspicuous advertising, was the excessive cost of these strictly imported goods, well out of the reach of most of China's billion women, who were forced to improvise using whatever materials were available to them, regardless of comfort or convenience.

These women didn't seem self-conscious though: as I waded between them to wash my hands they carried on talking over my head while wringing out terry towelling rags in the sink. I wondered if our obsessive British squeamishness concerning natural bodily functions wasn't weirder than this open confrontation of our femininity. Despite our rhetorical commitment to saving the bits of the planet we want to holiday in we insist on pumping waste sites full of diapers and sanitary towels: we'd run naked through our home town before flapping a cloth diaper on a washing-line or admitting that yes, we actually have voiding capabilities. Maybe the freedom promised by the tampax adverts was not the kind of liberation we really needed. I discussed my drive for a new openness concerning bodily functions with Laura but she returned me a scowl and a "don't think about it" kind of look. Not an open mind.

All those posters with the sparkly women bending backwards gave us an idea for our evening's entertainment. The term "acrobatics" is usually synonymous with Lenin, thick-necked women in spandex leotards and crushing humiliation in a too-tight gym skirt in front of 6th grade boys. So it was with enthusiasm that we booked our tickets for the legendary Shanghai Acrobatic Display. It was to be our goodbye to Shanghai. Little did we know we were to be the only spectators, apart from a swarm of Japanese tourists in identical seaside hats and matching camera cases who buzzed in ten minutes into the show and, ever fearful of personal space, squatted down right in front of us and began pouring each other's drinks. Their obsequiousness and general bobbing quite obstructed our view. Fortunately, there was little to see. The prize exhibit, a ragged looking Siberian Tiger, damaged the menacing reputation of big cats around the world by falling asleep on the job. The acrobats that followed were ingenious in their use of Grecian Urns and ardent in their recreation of ancient Egyptian legends in full costume (naturally this hindered the machinery of efficient tumbling), while girls in not-so-sparkly leotards disappeared through holes in barrels (the audience applauded but we weren't sure whether they cheered to see them go and come back, or just to go.) It seemed perhaps that it really was time for us to leave.

A TRIP ON A TRAIN

Five hours into our journey and we seemed to have amassed our usual crowd of curious spectators. Our impromptu ejection into the train from the arms of a burly station guard in a flurry of sweat, flying rucksack-straps and leaky water-bottles had probably accentuated our conspicuousness. Our reserved seats were occupied by a young man and woman so we hovered conspicuously in the middle of the carriage trying not to look at them. Eventually an older man stole a peek at our tickets and appealed to the hospitality of a small army of passengers (including three adventurous Japanese housewives with their Hello-Kitty lunchboxes and two elderly men with jamjars dangerously overfilled with tea) to stage an eviction. We felt quite dreadful. As we sank into our reclaimed seats to recoup our composure and dull our beetroot lustre w e realised what a commotion our entrance had caused. As far as we could see a sea of bobbing black heads all smoking or drinking or hawking watched us with that disinterested, unflinching curiosity that we had egoistically come to expect.

A man sitting opposite us in a smart tweed jacket launched into an animated spiel about our pending travel plans. He seemed to speak English better than he could understand it, and so gave us little opportunity to interject. It went along the lines of:

"No doubt you visit X. Let me tell you few things about X......... First thing to tell is that X boasts many X and X, and you should deliberately see X which I understand is very X". His meticulous narration working carefully through twenty-six potential destinations in strict alphabetical order helped pass the first hour of the trip. The tweed man then produced, with a theatrical flourish, a weighty tome entitled "Arc Welding - The Full Story". He proudly pointed out its 1961 publishing date and the carefully fingered "Oxford University Press" embossed on its spine. We nodded encouragingly as he opened it up and laid it on our laps for inspection. It was written in gloriously constipated Dickensian English compared with today's lax linguistic movements. Against every margin, he had carefully scribbled minute annotations in Chinese. It was grey with age and was evidently a sacred possession. We studied the finer details of spot welding with the appropriate aahs and oohs under his benevolent scrutiny, making every effort to get excited at the lines he personally highlighted for our inspection.

The elderly man with the full jam-jar, who had been wrenching his neck through a tortuous one hundred and eighty degrees to read our travel book, began to leaf through some colour postcards we'd bought in Shanghai. They were slowly circulated around the carriage in absolute silence, reverently passed between people with approving nods or slightly uncertain tilts of the head to the left or right. Occasionally someone would scratch hesitantly at the "paint" with a wondrous expression. We offered the elderly man our travel book to look through but he declined vehemently, flushed red and said "No English, No Read". Ten minutes later however, we noticed that the book was missing. Our friend had wedged it on his lap carefully hidden under the table and was rifling through the section detailing digestive ailments. He pointed conspiratorially to a couple of choice conditions and nodded violently while smiling his beautiful smile. We weren't sure whether he had these conditions or knew a man who did but we were careful not to share cutlery for the rest of the trip. Laura offered him a strange turd-like pill that we'd bought in Japan to clear up just the kind of problem the old man was alluding to. They smelt and tasted of creosote and came in a dark shade of faecal brown. Knowing they were completely "organic" did little to alleviate our uncertainty over their biological origins. Confusion then ensued as the gentleman pantomimed his way through two accurately -mimed options for consumption of the pill : the oral, or the suppositorial route to better health. Thank goodness he asked. He then rummaged through his bag and produced a pad of paper. From his expert drawings of handles and levers and knobs and switches we guessed he was in the fittings and fixtures business. We didn't know quite how to open a conversation about that one.

A man behind us then passed over the heads of the crowd the long side of a shoe box on which he'd drawn a portrait of Laura side on. We urged him to sign it but we took it away and thirty minutes later produced a picture of the station master (who kept offering us tea), the carriage attendant (who resurfaced every now and then to rifle through our postcards and study the pictures in our travel guide), and a young girl sitting next to him.

This fascination with Western published material was quite a consistent theme during our time in China. Everywhere we went people wanted to study our postcards, our handwriting, our books, stamps, magazines, letters. For years, Western publications, even Chinese books on the wrong topics, had been burnt or banned. Possessing the same could have dire consequences. This probably explains why our friends on the train flinched and clamoured to cram our books and postcards down the back of the seat when the station master first came in to our carriage.

IS THE ROOF LEAKING OR...?

We grabbed a three-wheeled motorised rickshaw from the station and shot off on a careering path dodging a volley of rotten fruit cast out from the back of the markets and a puddle of debris leaking from a large wooden apple cart that completely blocked the road. All around us the warm orange of brick glowed from walls and roofs, bathing the winding backstreets in a mist of rust-coloured heat. In every street women flaunted the latest fashion abomination from Beijing, transparent grease-proof frocks worn over over-sized floral knickers in psychedelic 1970's hues, that could be pulled up, it seemed, to double as ear-muffs. Like small barrage balloons, they trumpeted full of air with every step. In the scorching temperatures of Nanjing, that bellows-style undergarment must have provided precious ventilation.

Deciding to head to the China International Travel Service, we jogged unbecomingly alongside a bus and hailed questions at an inconspicuous looking man who seemed to be trying very hard to ignore us. He looked very harassed, not least because unbeknown to us, he was trying to conceal three crates of live fish under his seat. Our attention drew the attention of the driver, who threw the flustered looking man, complete with his fishy luggage, out onto the street. He was taking it all fairly well until he tripped over Laura's rucksack strap and sent half a crate of what appeared to be guppies under the bus. From the blur of faces the lined the pavement a barrage of people burst forth with a tumultuous roar and diving to their bellies started grabbing at the flapping fish. In the midst of this flurry of flapping kipper the agitated owner pantomimed to the driver that he must not move his bus or the fish would be squashed. Just as we wondered if all that China's stare squads were really waiting for was the derailing of a bucket of live fish, a man with an articulated vegetable cart appeared from a back alley with a mob of children and women flustering around his cart like disciplines following a new messiah. He drew his cart alongside our rucksacks, now drenched in fish, and hauled them onto his cart with a broad smile and a half-hearted cuff to a particularly tenacious little boy. We clambered in, gathering that he wanted to take us to CITS, and found a pleasant and comfy seat atop a small mound of melon pips.

Our lunch venue promised thirty-seven delicious menu items. Unfortunately thirty-six of them were out of season. Water-melon, surprisingly, was in season, and to our amazement had been crafted into a cunningly named cocktail called fruit koktak surprise which consisted of (here's the surprise!)nothing but melon and one tinned pineapple square (which we were told to share).

The CITS official could not understand our desire to reach Beijing by train. Have you ever been on a Chinese train? - he asked. "Rattle Rattle Rattle....." He began to convulse at an unnerving frequency of oscillation and we reached out our hands to provide immediate medical aid before realising he was impersonating a Chinese train. "We like it" we answered, but it didn't help us get tickets. It seemed the only option was for us to fly with China's National Airlines, Shanghai airlines. Open now to the possibility of imminent death we took what we still had of our lives and put them in the hand of a friendly man renting bicycles out of his rickshaw. Balancing with a rucksack was tricky but we made it back alive to the students' quarters of the University where our room, complete with straw mattress, single aeroplane propeller air-conditioning system and jug of cold water for bathing awaited us.

Feeling frivolous and wanting to wallow in a little of China's ancient exoticism, we bought tickets for a Chinese movie in which lots of women with log shaped hair-bands and unfeasibly long nails incited male passions to riot by bathing in baths of ass's milk at least seven times a day. Unfortunately our enjoyment of this cultural experience was marred by the immature phlegm -projecting skills of the row of men behind us. At first we thought the roof was leaking and plastered our bare legs with dainty pieces of Kleenex to stop the drips. Then we noticed an alarming correlation between the splat of that curiously *sticky?* water and a loud hawking sound which we heard, on average, point eight seconds earlier. Liberally pasted with musical phlegm bullets for two whole hours, we finally conceded defeat in the final hour when those little protein-packed parcels started landing on our arms and neck. Enough culture for one day.

ISN'T THAT
ROCHDALE COMMUNITY CENTRE?

Today's ambitious sight-seeing plans deteriorated into a tour of chickens. In fact, the worst chickens in the whole world. Prominent in today's celebrity line-up were a chicken (who appeared to be named Malcolm, we weren't quite sure) sitting very placidly at a Buddhist monastery with his feet tied together on a washing line tether, a cluster of three disreputable-looking chickens sitting in the back of a cycle-taxi, an impertinent looking chicken peeping out from a lady's handbag, half a chicken (an astonishing lack of feathers on its lower body) sitting on a bald man's shoulder, and a bright green chicken sitting on top of a radio set in a posh department store.

We started our morning by inspecting our bicycles in the cold light of day. Laura's saddle was wrapped in black bin bags and was tilted vertically to a forty-five degree angle, which would seriously limit her chances of ever having children. Mine had no brakes. Conspicuous in the daylight, we now attracted an alarmingly mobile swarm of stare-squaddies who followed us round the streets on their bicycles. Naturally this caused some confusion when we turned and they didn't. Fortunately there are a million times more bikes than cars here so their is some authority in being on two wheels instead of four, but the hurtling by of large articulated trucks was still unnerving.

We rode out on our bikes to a place called The Drum Tower, a huge fourteenth century monument decorated in the ubiquitous plum and mango colours of imperial China. Inside, it housed one large drum surrounded by a number of Neolithic speakers and a tower of stacked-up benches. No one seemed impressed by the drum. In one corner a group of pop-sock sporting women played mah-jong, in the other three policeman supped Snappy C from trendy glass bottles.The rooms at the bottom of the tower were redolent of English churches and I loitered for a while under the low-stone doorways imbibing nostalgic smells of mediaeval England.

Leaving the Drum Tower, we found ourselves running a gauntlet of beggars, the first we had really encountered so far on our trip. All old men, with rattling enamel mugs and sad eyes whitened by glaucoma.

Parking our bikes, we negotiated an argument with an officious lady who claimed to be the "bicycle protection fee collector". At four feet five inches tall, she was quite formidable. Laura was paralysed with fear and would have signed over her life if not heavily supervised. Finally we agreed on a nominal fee and she shuffled off with a hrrrmphh. The pagoda was ten stories high and as we climbed the endless spiral of slipper-smooth stairs we were treated to a small vignette of human tragedy unfolding on every storey. We just glimpsed it, flashing through, like stills from some disjointed German movie. On floor one, a policewoman sobbed uncontrollably into the arms of a colleague, on floor two, a young couple necked by the light of a computer game that the male necker was still managing to play despite the inconvenient tryst, on floor three, Laura's baseball cap very unfortunately flew off the side of the pagoda, which was a more auspicious end than it deserved, on floor four six square inches of ancient plum-coloured paint dissolved under an ill-aimed slop from my sprite can........ We only made it to floor five, where two young men seemed to be fighting in the doorway, before turning back.

Back on the ground, we dodged another protection racketeer, who seemed to be offering protection against the original bicycle protection-fee lady. Laura was prepared to pay whatever it took. (I wondered what unfortunate childhood memories this tiny, officious woman had unearthed in Laura's psyche). Fortunately our bicycles were still there and in one piece so we sped off, but not before a man offered us a "mysterious adventure" on his magic bus. Surprisingly we declined, and headed out of town, way way out of town to see Hong Ku's tomb. We flagged down a man to ask directions. "No problem" he said, leaping back on his bike and leading us like some heavenly missionary through the clamour and clatter of the crazy streets and out, out of town on a serene lane where scenes of rural country life unfolded in the fields and hedgerows flanking the road. Brick farmhouses flanked the road, with calves and ponies tied outside. People washed their clothes in the stream running along the road. It reminded me the kind of quaint scene of rural life and industry that pompous Victorian writers were so quick to eulogise.

It was about ten kilometres each way, and our bikes were designed for neither comfort or speed. Occasionally our guide would turn and raise his thumb - "OK?". Fearful of offending someone with an inappropriate western hand-gesture, I touched my finger to my ear lobe. I was sure I had read somewhere that this meant "good". He immediately squealed his bike to a stop, almost derailing Laura in the process, and leant over towards me with a loud "**O-K-?**", carefully enunciating every syllable. Yes, I replied, humbly, "OK" .

The road leading up to the tomb was flanked by imperious looking horses, lions and soldiers. It would have been a scary place at night. Our kindly guide stopped and after rinsing his towel carefully in a water -fountain gave it us to wipe our sweaty brows with. He then produced a huge black fan from his bag and a jar of green tea with three little plastic cups. Unsure how to reciprocate, we bought him a Coca-Cola, which he held awkwardly for a few minutes. Tactfully we turned our backs for a moment and when we turned round the glass was empty. We all tried to ignore the little puddle leaking from the shrubbery behind him.

We tried to communicate through the shared language of Kanji, the pictographic symbols adopted by the Chinese and later imported to Japan. As usual though, he was more interested in the English text in our guide book and spent quite a while poring over the photographs and chuckling at the pictures. He then produced a book full of gorgeous pen and ink drawings of pine forests and farm-houses, apparently a collection of his works. Just in the middle of our genuinely impressed coos and aahs, an ant crawled up my trainer. He spotted it with eagle eyes and before I could swat it away, he was stamping out all the ants in the vicinity with a maniacal gleam in his eyes.

We never really heard him speak, except for a few huffs when eradicating the ant kingdom, but he was a wonderful, helping, obliging companion. We never did find out what he'd been doing when we abducted him but as we waved him off into the setting sunlight we felt certain we'd meet him again. It was astonishing how, despite the phenomenal number of people we had seen, and would see, in China, we had never once felt threatened or intimidated or in any kind of danger, except perhaps of hysteria, spontaneous digestive implosion or an ugly road traffic fatality.

Time was getting on so we didn't actually go into the Tomb, which was decorated in an over-bold mango-plum-cocktail combination, reminiscent, Laura remarked absently, of Rochdale community centre. I somehow did not think that was what the imperial tomb designers had been aiming for. We headed back on our bicycles, enjoying a more leisurely pace without our guide, to find that the man who'd taken the deposit for our bicycles had gone home. His colleague was not allowed to give us back our deposit as it wasn't his job. We could see it sitting on a chair in a neat little envelope on which we'd written our names but he couldn't hand it over. This was the Communist one man-one job system at its pinnacle of inflexibility. There seemed little sense in creating a commotion about the equivalent of one US dollar. Nor did we want to get this man, who was very friendly and helpful in every other way, in trouble. In the end we left the envelope behind.

A TRIP TO MR SONG'S HOUSE

The next morning we decided to pay a visit to Mr Song, the man we had met on the train. His house was nestled in a burrow of winding streets behind the parks that flanked the city centre. It looked small by Western standards, three rooms perhaps. The walls were a brilliant egg-shell white, covered with calligraphy scrolls and translucent Chinese landscapes. In China calligraphy is considered the highest visual artform. "I couldn't practice my calligraphy for many years", said Mr Song, "and I never got my skill back". He invited us to sit on a low wooden couch while he made the tea, which was served in sturdy porcelain cups with lids to keep the heat in. He'd lived here apparently for over ten years. "Why couldn't you paint?" asked Laura.

"It's a long story." He settled down with his tea. " The country was in ruins, of course, after Chiang Kai Shek fled to Taiwan with the country's gold reserves, but everyone was fired up, excited to be helping to build the New China. There was such a spirit of unity and we all worked together to get China back on the map. Mao was such a hero, you cannot understand today how there could be such a hero. When he unveiled his plans for The Great Leap Forward, we all rushed around collecting pots to smelt into armaments. My mother even gave up her jewellery and my father sat up all night polishing his trophies before sending them to the refineries. Of course, in the end, it was disastrous, while we collected iron there was famine in the fields. Millions died, you know. It damaged Mao for ever, some say.

"Certain people in the government, some say, took advantage of the disasters to promote their own power. They sowed the seeds for the cultural revolution which would follow. They invented and regulated China's bureaucratic system but Mao controlled the army. Mao denounced all their ideas as capitalist and revisionist, and announced a nation-wide program to struggle against those who were in authority and exploiting the masses. His own ideas, called "*Mao Tsedong thought*", were to guide the Revolution. All the old ideas of class, culture and custom, would be wiped out, and all Mao's opponents sent to the countryside for education. They burnt all my books and paintings. They destroyed the theatres, the universities, thousands of years of learning. Only art which served the revolution was permitted".

"What about the Red Guards? Were they part of the Cultural Revolution?"

"Not at first. Mao didn't seem to know when he recognised the first Red Guards what terror they would unleash. After all they were just schoolchildren really. But once it all started, he seemed to see it as a tool, a weapon he could use to bring down teachers and professors and doctors. There were no rules for the Red Guards, no one stopped them doing what they wanted to do. It was a hideous time. "

"What happened to you, during the cultural revolution?"

"Oh. Many many things. I was working as a teacher then and like so many of my colleagues they sent me to the country-side to be re-educated. I was so sick there, I couldn't work, but they made me go to the fields every day to stand up to my knees in water. We were lucky though, down in the south where the fields were still full. Up in the north, many people died eating grass and tubers or froze on the hills where they scrabbled for roots in the snow. "

"What happened to your father?"

"They denounced him. He had fought for Chiang Kai Shek, and now he owned lands in his old home-land Sichuan which made him a landlord. In the town hall they held struggle sessions to get him to confess to his crimes. The Red Guards tied his hands together and kicked him through the streets. He tried to think what they wanted him to confess but it was never enough. The took him into prison and kept him awake for days on end and beat him when he fell asleep. Eventually my mother got a letter saying he'd died from an infection he'd picked up in prison. She heard from another prisoner's wife that he'd died many months before. My mother thinks they tortured him. She wasn't allowed to see him after he went into prison, though she travelled there, a hundred miles, every week until they changed her work unit and sent her to the country-side. There was nothing we could do in those days, there was no justice system, no system for placing complaints. No one, so far as we know, ever investigated what really happened to my father.

"I was released in 1975. They moved me to a factory nearer to my mother where I worked making bricks for another five years. We were lucky, at least we could be close together."

It is curious how one's definition of luck is so relative.

"Is it dangerous for you to be talking to us?".

"Maybe. Even after the massacre in Tiananmen Square, we were followed to make sure we didn't speak to journalists or westerners who might take news back to the rest of the world."

"It was a great tragedy" we nodded.

"Yes. But there have been many worse tragedies in China's history that the West did not care about. The difference with this one is there were photographs, western reporters were there, word got out. There were monetary ties between the two countries. It was your obligation to cry out against the action but it does not mean your countries really care about China's people, they just care about how they will look in the eyes of the rest of the world."

It was time for us to go. The sun was settling down behind the trees in the park. We thanked Mr Song for his time and his hospitality and the lessons we'd learnt about China and her long and troubled history. It was extraordinary for us, living in a society that knew almost no fear, to imagine the constant threat of persecution that had stalked almost a quarter of the world's population for so much of this century. A knock at the door for us meant flowers or friends or someone campaigning for charity. In China it could mean the last time a man saw his family. I still think of that whenever I go to answer my door.

THE FLIGHT OF ALMOST CERTAIN DEATH
WILL DEPART FROM GATE C...

"Snappy C?" invited the seating air-hostess with unnerving undertones of panic in her voice. We shake our heads. "Sandwich?". She produced a film-wrapped package of squished bread and butter laced with slivers of an unidentifiable vegetable product. We shook our heads again. "Peach Juice?". We were saved from further interrogation by the overhead tanoy system which crackled into life with a rip of static electricity. The Captain launched into a high-pitched, monotonous rhetoric which incited all the Chinese passengers around us to riot. People started clambering up from their seats, cups of snappy C abandoned in the rush. Used to being the last ones to get a good joke, we looked around in bewilderment. The overhead tanoy coughed hesitantly into life again and the Captain, in a voice tinged liberally now with hysteria, scrambled, in English: "THE ENGINE IS BAD, THE ENGINE IS BAD, EVACUATE THE PLANE". His voice seemed to fade away towards the end and we imagined him climbing out of his cockpit as he shouted into the microphone. We were the only people still sitting in the plane.

We should have seen it coming. Sitting in the plane, nervously awaiting take-off, fanning ourselves with our inflight safety cards, we traded premonitions, thinking to cheat fate by launching a pre-emptive first strike to derail his fateful machinations. We laughed at our own devil-may-care-ness and chewed our nails between sips of a carbonated hyperactivity-inducing non-fruit product. Funny how we had been taxiing for so long, we observed, trying to ignore the asthmatic whine of the engine and that unnerving clank that seemed to originate right under our seats. Despite the imperious glares we directed at where we imagined the back of the Captain's head would be (later we calculated we'd been staring out the microwave) we continued to taxi, round and round and round. Despite Laura's palpable hyperventilation and the torrent of sweat that ran down our faces, things seemed fairly calm. The man next to me drew out a small pocket donkey-Kong game and starting clicking as if sheer mental energy and lots of beeping would get us into the air.

Just then a fleet of anxious looking air-hostesses swarmed out from the cockpit with stiff, over-reassuring smiles and carcinogenic sandwiches stacked up like a bounty-hunter's booty in a strange orange plastic bag. They bullied us mercilessly with artificial drink choices and bags of curiously-green peanuts while calculating the minutes to our certain death. Then came the in-flight safety announcement, manic like a record on fast-play, exhorting us all to flee with our lives. Grown men were put back in touch with their bodily functions; "machine" and "evacuate" were added to our check-list of vital foreign phrases.

We clamoured down the emergency stairs and almost collapsed as the sweltering forty degree heat hammered down on our pasty shoulders. Shade was a long long way away. Around us the runway stretched in every direction, shimmering with heat-haze. "RUN" shouted someone. It could have been the captain. We hauled our hand luggage behind us by the straps as we lurched across the bumpy concrete field, wondering between asthmatic gulps whether instantaneous combustion would have been speedier than heart failure.

Back in the lounge, the air-hostesses came round again proffering the by-now squishier vacuum-wrapped green sandwiches and some cartons of peach juice that had been salvaged from the plane. Mine had a footprint on it. A large Swedish man came over to sit with us and told us quite confidently that it could take a week to get a replacement part. "Its an American plane" he informed us. "Could take for ever". "Thank goodness you are not on a Russian plane. Then it would be —— " He made a pleasant gesture of wiping an imaginary blade across his throat. He seemed quite cheerful for a Swede. "Hmmmmm" was all we could think up in response. The policeman lounged indolently around, mockingly untroubled by our plight as they reclined with their pop-socked feet propped up on the conveyor belt that was the security and immigration office all rolled into one.

An hour later, the stiff-faced air hostesses invited us with a sweeping hand-gesture to re-board flight A45 to Beijing. It was an exact re-run of our first embarkation: we took the same seats and went through the same pantomimed safety procedures. From our window seats in the lounge we had seen no one approach, let alone give a full mechanical overhaul to, flight A45 bound for Beijing. Laura by now was convinced that this is some kind of money-making scam designed to separate us from our baggage.

The overhead tanoy coughs back into life and the Captain announces in shaky English "ENGINE REPAIRED. PREPARE TO FLY. ENGINE REPAIRED. PREPARE TO FLY." And we start to taxi. And taxi. And taxi some more. Until again, again we cry, the captain shakily informs us that THE ENGINE IS BAD. This time we take our cue from the rapidly fleeing Chinese passengers and hear his announcement as we lunge out the door. An unusually large Chinese lady unleashes a massive static build-up from her polyester frock as she lands on my head. There is no time to look for an exit wound as we limp across the runway, eyebrows smoking and bladders quivering from the unexpected impact.

Another two hours pass in the lounge, during which time no-one approaches the plane. The Swedish man is talking to himself in a corner so we give him a wide berth. Someone comes round selling plastic trinkets, a small child vomits on my shoe and a bird flies into the safety glass. Time literally flies and before we can play another exciting round of eye-spy, we are invited by a disinterested looking policeman with a baton to re re-board for a third time. The air-hostesses are looking pretty frazzled by this time and wear wary scowls in place of their former stiff smiles. Back on board they bring round small plastic shoulder massagers which would not be out of place in an X-rated catalogue. Perceptively they picked up that we were a little frazzled; in desperate times in China small hand-held vibrators are obviously easier to procure than a full mechanical overhaul.

Twenty minutes of anxious taxiing pass during which everyone clutches their hand luggage and keeps one foot pointed towards the emergency exit. The captain seems to cough occasionally into the microphone which incites us all to general panic. I suspect he is having a private joke at our expense and half-expect Jeremy Beadle to pop out with a microphone from the ladies toilet. Just as hysteria finally threatens to overtake us, the engine makes one extra-large groan and we feel the ground drop away beneath us. It takes us by surprise, and luggage flies everywhere as the over-head compartments empty over the already jumpy passengers. Poised for another emergency evacuation, none of us have our seat-belts on and small children start rolling around in the aisles. But we are in the air. The take-off is bumpy, and several people start to scream but we are flying. Almost everyone orders a beer at the earliest opportunity. The man opposite us sternly informs us that beer is not a drink for women but by this time our desire to accommodate to cultural convention has all but withered away. We put on out headphones to drown out the sound of his Donkey Kong game and settle down to watch an eerily prophetic disaster movie on the inflight entertainment system.

WHAT WAS I DOING
TWO HUNDRED YEARS AGO?

Surprisingly, Beijing is full of Italians. Conspicuous in sagging platform shoes and designer shades they commandeer key landmarks for endless photoshoots that invariably end up in tears. Only in China, it seemed, would gaudy Italian fashion find an admiring market of beautiful young women with a penchant for gold-coated plastic accessories. Indeed, I wondered if the whole shower-cap thing couldn't be somehow traced back to the Italians. After all, all those curly-headed naked statues showering in forest gullies. Curl control would surely have been a valid concern of the early Greek demi-god.

There were Italians on our bus to the Summer Palace, which was a shame. Otherwise, however, the trips were pleasant. I say trips because every time we hit a red traffic light (apparently a fairly new weapon in China's traffic discipline armament) the bus would stop, never to start again. We would have to wait for a new bus to come along and jump-start our engine. Of course at each red light the driver would roll further and further forward to avoid stopping until we were sticking right out in the middle of the road. All the people at the front of the bus would race to the back with a frenzied squeal. Laura and I got a lot of Chinese bottoms on our laps. I pictured the front of the bus rearing up like an angry centipede, its bald tires spinning impotently as we ground the back of the bus into the road. In all, we stopped eleven times between leaving Beijing and arriving at the Summer Palace. It was a long ride.

The Palace itself was eerily evocative of a time we couldn't possibly have known (though I asked myself some pretty searching questions about my previous lives.) Decked in the ubiquitous plum and mango hues of Imperial China with magnificently detailed friezes in cobalt blue and iron red the Palace was not one single monument but a collection of buildings favoured by the Manchu Court for summer retreats. Women with log-like contraptions in their hair and unfeasibly long finger-nails tottered around in sheath-like dresses. They carried authentic period-loudspeakers that suffused the beautiful afternoon breeze with the atmospheric crackle of static electricity. In some of the courtyards you could dress up in period costume (including the amazing log-head device) and have your photograph taken with a wax statue of the late Empress Wu Cixi. To our amazement, these little photo pagodas, complete with two dimensional cut-outs of 19th century court maidens that you could put your head through, were completely overrun with Japanese tourists. One young man from rural Tohoku took quite a shine to a wet-nurse's frock with leg of mutton sleeves but their ten minute tour was up. He looked rather sad as they piled him back into the bus.

Along the edge of the lake ran The Long Corridor, which, surprisingly, is a long corridor. 738 metres long to be precise with over 800 individually hand-painted ceiling friezes built into the roof. It was quite magnificent. One the other side of the Palace grounds, reached only by hundreds of treacherously uneven steps, The Temple of the Fragrance of Buddha waited patiently in the shadow of the mountainside. Despite its whimsical title, the Temple was fringed by three thousand empty carbonated fruit product cans. Inside the Temple a magnificent gold Buddha with a thousand mythological arms and twelve faces reclined against a backdrop of seascapes and painstakingly hand-painted mini-Buddhas. My favourite spot though, above the Temple of The Fragrance of Buddha, was the Hall of Dispelling Vapours, one of the few authentic and original monuments left on the site (most of the original palace had been destroyed by Anglo-French forces in 1876 and painstakingly rebuilt in later years). The elaborate gold plasterwork, and intricate lime and mango coloured ceramic tiles flanking every wall settled into my memory to be unearthed two years later when I finally visited India. All around the temple craggy rocks magnificently hewn from the mountainside and cast about idled in the oppressive afternoon sun. Below us, the mountain receded into the murmuring oblivion of a heat haze that nibbled at the outlines of the junk ships trawling through the lake's jade-green waters. From our vantage point above the Cloud-Relieving Pavilion, we could see figures splashing and swimming in the waters. We finally felt we were in the China our romantic imaginations still clung to.

THE NEAREST WE GET TO A DATE
IN ALL OUR TRAVELS

That evening we visited one of Beijing's most notorious eateries (the marriage between food and notoriety is not necessarily a blessed one in China), a grand theatrical place redolent of some of the scarier scenes of The Cook, The Thief, His Wife and Her Lover, (but fortunately not the part where they eat that unsuspecting naked man). The interior was cast in a sinister red glow that brought back all those childhood nightmares surrounding the meat-like slabs of marble in Cruella de Ville's parlour. (Later on in our trip, in the backwaters of Outer Mongolia, we'd find such elegant lighting used to a very sinister effect. But that story will come.) While we slummed it in the main hall with its adornments of marble and alabaster and endless Greek columns, the upper echelons of Chinese society feasted on chicken entrails and crystal duck's tongue delivered on solid gold platters.

Our waiter appraised us carefully while taking our order as if evaluating our potential monetary worth. He materialised five minutes later with a fat smile, shepherding two unfeasibly tall albino men in obscenely tight cycling shorts in front of him with a long carving fork. Edited highlights from the film swam dizzyingly back into my mind. "Two men. Two women. Luckeeeeee!" he announced with a stern nod and a dazzling smile, prodding the men into the two seats opposite us.

"We are Swedish" whispered the blonder, taller man apologetically. We nodded sympathetically. If we felt conspicuous with our breasts and hairy ankles these man mountains must be ready to tar and feather themselves. At least that's what depressed Swedish people always seemed to do in Ingmar Bergman movies. The Swedes seemed rather sullen. Dunking their limp duckless pancakes (they were vegetarians) in the delectable hoi-sin sauce they explained despondently how much they were enjoying China. They were a little concerned about the attention they seemed to be attracting from village women. Given the relative inadequacy of their cycling shorts and the singular conspicuousness of such garments in communist China, I felt the attention was likely warranted. Many years later my husband would plan a lycra-wrapped tour of China based solely on their success with far less spectacular results. Interestingly the shorter one (all things being relative) launched into an animated conversation about the cucumber price-war currently raging "like a plague" through the Swedish highlands. Apparently, prices upwards of one British Pound per inch length had been reported. He explained, lest we feel sufficiently outraged to mount some kind of indignant protest, that these were rumours were strictly unauthenticated. His friend nodded gravely. I had heard that there was little to do during the long Swedish winters but even so this national obsession with fresh produce seemed strangely displaced. The taller Swede was an auditor. His friend was something big in road sign design but we couldn't quite settle on a job description. Just at that moment the waiter resurfaced and suggested without a hint of self-consciousness that we should all go home and start producing "eggs". The lanky Swedes departed in a blur of white hair and hairless cheekbones.

We were not alone for long. Our waiter, affronted at the insult these vegetarian Vikings had dealt us, magiced up a tiny little Singaporean for our amusement. He was quite overcome with excitement. He divulged his life history to us over some disembodied duck part, practically prostrate on the table as he whispered conspiratorially to us about his wife's monthly mood-swings and in-store spending account. He made an exaggerated show of propriety whenever the waiter came swinging gaily by, conspicuously changing the conversation to feature some hot-on-the-market gardening accessory. (He was something big in the garden centre industry). We were fascinated by the relentless advance of the soy sauce soaking up his tie and into the creases of his jacket cuff as he leaned across the table. Interestingly, he explained how the Singaporeans, despite their widely recognised contempt for Chinese people, food, officialdom, politics, lifestyle, language and chickens, regard China as the Motherland. He spoke seven languages, English, Cantonese, Mandarin, three local Chinese dialects and Malay. Chinese people were fairly disgusting he explained, fishing a piece of gizzard out from between his teeth with his cuff-link, but there was a deep cultural and spiritual connection between the two countries. Of course Singapore was an exotic melting pot of culture and commerce and China was something of a rural cess-pit, but the Chinese, he argued strongly, could not be held accountable for their lack of business acumen or appalling social policy because the system was intrinsically flawed. He waved his finger at us to emphasise his point, showering his shirt-front with tiny shards of duck. People could not be expected to fight a system that only rewards corruption, he cautioned. Just at that moment, he felt the first salty sting of soy seeping through his jacket cuff and leapt off with a squeal and a suspicious scowl as us (as if we'd known!) to hose himself down.

DO YOU THINK
WE'RE INCOMPETENT OR SOMETHING?

Its was a curious place, that hotel we stayed in. The female proprietor seemed vehemently contemptuous towards foreigners and their ridiculous ways, which was ironic as the whole hotel seemed populated largely by Scandinavians, except for a family of seven Lebanese men, who made the daily ritual of filing past our bedroom door in their underpants something of a pilgrimage. The male proprietor made a proper show of avoiding us dairy-infested hairballs when his wife was around but while she laid down for her afternoon nap (with a little aeroplane sleeping- mask over her eyes) he would cycle round the rooms proffering all kinds of dodgy black market money-changing propositions. In Beijing the most common greeting we heard was "Change Money" - "Change Money?" .Indeed, today we stopped a policeman in the street to ask him where the Bank of China had disappeared to (buildings have a habit of spontaneously evaporating in this curious place). With a surreptitious nod and wink (we thought he was having some kind of seizure) he made a conspicuous show of switching off his walkie-talkie and putting his finger to his lips before tip-toeing over to his sentry box in exaggerated slow-motion. He looked quite conspicuous, even for a policeman. Expecting to be booked for having body hair or pimples, we were quite surprised when he drew out a small Hello Kitty purse (evidently confiscated from a Japanese tourist) and offered "You Change Money?". We declined.

We had to get over that day to the Qiaoyuan hotel where Mark's alter ego, a sardonic French-Canadian called Lou, exhorted money from innocent travellers in exchange for train tickets. Lou would take our passports and would procure our Mongolian visas the next day for a paltry 28US$. It all seemed too easy and we had until five o'clock to get there. Given that time was on our side, there was no keeping us out of the Friendship store, where all kinds of Western and Chinese luxury commodities could be procured for hard currency. Despite the thin chance we had of reaching it alive, given Laura's anvil-shaped saddle and my less than symmetrical handlebars, the lure of real Cadbury's chocolate and a drink that wasn't fizzy could not be ignored. Laura fell for a red silk sheath dress that looked quite beautiful on her slim figure. Given the indignity of trying it on on the shop floor, with an over-eager little man pressing against her to pop her poppers every other second, and the sarcastic remarks of a couple of conspicuously blue-haired old ex-pats who couldn't have fitted into that dress with a crow-bar and a bucket of Vaseline, Laura more than deserved the dress. If I didn't discover that very moment that my money belt was ominously unzipped and half my American dollars missing, I would have bought if for her myself.

I wondered if my belt had been rifled on the bus, a notorious site, we later learned, for pick-pockets to work, given the endless jostling of people and the tendency of most passengers to enter a kind of hypnotic state until with uncanny accuracy, they awake just in time to get off. Fortunately, we hastily counted up what money we had left, and were relieved to see that we just had enough to pay for our Mongolian visas and breathed a sigh of relief, for the short-term at least.

We set out in a leisurely fashion, weaving our bikes through the throng of clattering cranking engines that muddied the Beijing air. Suddenly we seemed to hit something like the London rush hour. Out of nowhere, thousands of bikes came hurtling down on us from side alleys and backstreets. Desperately trying to keep our heads and wheels together in the jangling mesh of metal and rubber that ensued we careered around huge wooden carts drawn by three horses, men with upwards of thirty live chickens dangling, blinking, from the mudguards of motorcycle combination cars, madmen driving pedicabs with ice-cream-van style frills and Hollywood style movie bulletins flapping from their bumpers. Floundering as we stumbled onto a building site that seemed to be excavating pure asbestos from the ground along the banks of a muddy looking canal, we woke a man who was sleeping in the back of his truck. It was astonishing where people managed to sleep in China. Road workers curled up alongside throbbing pneumatic drills, pedi-cab drivers clambered onto their warm bonnets to take a nap, shop assistants dropped their heads onto the counters, policemen managed to somehow wedge themselves upright in their little sentry-box stations and catch a nap behind their impenetrable visors. This particular man awoke with a jump murmuring something about ducks and making some impotent kung-fu style gesture with his right arm. He looked at us in curiosity then started calling in panic for his friends. We backed off, not realising how scary we had come to look with our wayward curls and cavernous pores. We offered him five Yuan to show us where the Qiaoyuan hotel was and he leapt into his truck and drove off into the dust. Laura, a better woman than I held chase for ten minutes and probably longer, but my lungs muddied quickly with all the dust in the air and I had to stop for a rest. As soon as I started up again, I realised that I was hopelessly, inextricably lost, and that Laura held our map in her backpack. Furthermore, I had the passports in my money-belt. If we didn't get the passports to Lou tonight, our whole trip was doomed. Tomorrow he was out of the office all day winging dodgy immigration scams and the next day we were due to board our train to nowhere .

Fired by sheer panic, I embarked on a frantic bicycle dash through a catacomb of backstreets fronted by dingy green cafes with yellowing plastic tables, past old men sitting on their haunches playing dominoes next to trolleys laden up with fruit, past children playing with dead animals in the gutter, past women squatting in the streets to take a crap and past mad old men in flamboyant floral underwear. It was crazy, the world seemed to be coming at me head-on. My arm ached from the perpetual effort of trying to keep my handlebars straight, and my spine felt as if it was hammering through concrete like a pneumatic drill. Between flashes of pain and inspiration, I wondered if Laura was all right. I had been so frantic in my merry helser flight of certain death through Beijing's backstreets that I had forgotten to worry if she was alive and well or crushed beneath the wheels of a truck. Perhaps that man had abducted her and holed her up in some little sweat shop to treadle her life away at a loom like a curly Mancunian Rapunzel. In my heart I hoped her tucked up in a little cafe somewhere sipping real filter coffee (though uncharitably I had to concede there would be a certain injustice in that).

Just at that moment, to my utter amazement, I pulled out in front of a massive dormitory style building with the letters spelling Qiaoyuan Hotel pinned in a wonky kind of line along its grey concrete walls. I dashed in through the main doors in a heightened state of panic. The digital clock on the wall menaced me with its sharp ticks and almost seemed to smirk as it turned five right there in front of me. Frantically I rifled through my money belt before realising that Laura had the room number we needed scribbled on the map. I had no idea how to explain in Chinese what I wanted. Just as I resigned myself to never sleeping in a yurt, a familiar face sprung out at me from the stairwell. It was the man we'd woken up nearly two hours ago to help us find the hotel. Asking no questions, I responded to his urgent hand gestures with a fast tripping pace up the stairs and collapsed, wheezing and pink as a very hot beetroot through a deceptively dark office doorway. Coolly, I missed the step and tumbled in head-first banging my head on a Mexican flower pot. A man with dyed-blonde hair sneered with at me with half his face from behind a desk liberally adorned with photos of himself in various stages of albinism (because, obviously, bleaching your hair is a very important journey of self-discovery.) He looked a bit like a cockatoo. This was our first meeting with Lou. He checked his watch with a facetious scowl. "Nice of you to join us". Us? Us? I turned around and saw Laura skulking in the shadow of a trifidic cheese plant. While Lou coolly extracted the last of our remaining hard currency and confiscated our passports, we beamed to see each other again. As we left his office he murmured something about trying not to get lost between Tuesday and Thursday, when our train was due to leave. This was too much for Laura, who asked him in great indignation "Do you think we're incompetent or something?" To his credit, at least he had the decency to be honest. "Yes" he said, after a misleading moment's hesitation. It was a shame we'd ever have to see him again.

Peter Ustonov told us all about The Forbidden City...

The Great Wall of China without its legendary camels!

A beautiful Mongolian yurt in the Gobi Desert...

Paying respects at the Temple, Ulan Bator.

Posing Fonz-style in Ulan Bator's main town square...

**Despite the crowds, we battled across the main city platz in
search of beetroot.**

A dust cloud brewing over the Gobi Desert.

A Mongolian horseman goes galloping by, smiling despite the saddle...

He watched himself put the head back on the goat and run backward around the meadow. Then waited for an explanation...

In the back streets of Hong Kong, carrying chickens to the market.

Watching the sun come up on a slow boat to China.

Washing in a stopcock
in Shanghai's
backstreets.

We met this family in
Shanghai. Surpris-
ingly a small family of
piglets were hiding
out in the back of the
sidecar.

People produced all manner of unexpected rainwear from their pockets...

Preparing for a night at Beijing's opera.

Navigating the animal, vegetable, mineral maze of Shanghai's backstreets on our boneshakers...

Ulan Bator, Outer Mongolia. The only remaining Buddhist Temple in the area. The monks did a wonderful job of ignoring our psychedelic rainwear despite the incessant flashing of our cameras.

A monk weaves his way through an army of pigeons to morning prayer little suspecting we had been trailing him for some time.

Despite not sharing one mutually intelligible word, we pantomimed our excitement at being admitted into the Buddhist Temple.

The houses in Siberia were low, hewn from precariously stacked piles of logs trussed together with a cunning mesh of rope and some kind of congealed potato product.

A young boy struts before an ominously graphic 'danger' poster at a Siberian station. Malcolm had traded his baseball cap for a punnet of raspberries.

A water-wheel in Siberia.

People burst forth from derelict railway carriages to sell us potatoes and raspberries wrapped in newspaper. Food had never tasted so good.

"The more I study this picture, the more this Siberian house
looks too small and the tree too big!"

--*Kirsti*

St. Basil's Cathedral, Red Square. A giant tropical fruit salad of a Church with its pineapple spikiness and the apple-like roundness of its nine towers.

THE GREAT WALL OF CHINA

That morning we took a tour to see the Great Wall of China. The bus driver sat us next to a pink-faced pair of young Chinese men who shuffled awkwardly in their seats, a quiver of desperation twitching in their lower lips as we flung ourselves down beside them. One sported a kind of Mohican haircut. From the look on his face I wondered if his friends had got him drunk one night and done it to him while he was sleeping. We offered them a piece of the dry-looking cake that we'd salvaged from the breakfast table that morning, which seemed to break the ice. I was surprised that The Great Wall, the most tangible and enduring symbol of China's grand imperial history, had survived the purges of the Cultural Dissolution movement when so many monuments were torn down or at least defiled in some permanent way. The boy without the Mohican haircut said, to my surprise, "They had the right idea in some ways. Now everyone is obsessed by money - " he paused the punch a few buttons on his Casio wrist-watch - "there is no sense of honour or unity, we are all after quick riches. No one really cares any more about China". Given what Mr Song had told us, I was quite taken aback.

"But what about all the struggles, the imprisonments, the re-education, the endless eating of tubers?".

"I don't really know much about all that. But how bad could it have been. Look at all the gains we made in that time. Maybe those people were happy to die for a cause they believed in." His friend chipped in. "There are no causes anymore. You Americans (!!) get all excited about human rights in China but most of us do O.K." He fingered the strap on his Head sportswear bag. "Its not so bad here." He stopped to think for a moment, looking tragic and persecuted with his budgie-like hairstyle. "Is it true there's a new Sega game system coming out with seventeen extra speed options?"

We were fortunate in going to a recently exposed section of the Wall that had suffered very little tourist traffic to date. It looked almost lonely up there, high on the hill, deprived these days of marauding

Mongol scouts to menace with its arrow slits and sturdy stones. Sadly the commercially adroit Chinese Authorities for the Authentic Preservation of Old Monuments had seen fit to install a slightly asthmatic chair lift to carry tourists to the top. Lofty environmental ideals aside, we would willingly have sunk into its padded vinyl comforts. But we had forgotten all our money, which made us stupid to start with. Now it made us hot, sweaty and stupid as we climbed a vertical cliff-face for thirty minutes in our flip-flops.

When we finally reached the first reassuring stones, we were so used to looking down during our climb that the bright light of the sky dizzied us. The wall seemed to tower imperiously over mountains that spilled like a sheet of crumpled green satin as far as the eye could see. There were turrets and watchtowers and huge flights of stone steps which made us dizzy to the point of passing out going down and up. We met a Dutch couple who were taking three months off work to explore China. "It's hard" said Anneka, "the constant staring, the endless chicken, the lack of privacy". "We nearly went home a few weeks ago," said William, "it was all getting too much. But now we've got a second wind, we'll make it through the three months, we can do it....." He looked a little uncertain. I realised that we were making such a whirlwind trip. For people who were here for longer, each day spent here must bring new frustrations. "You are honeymooning right now" said William with a hint of envy. "But soon you will want to go home". Home was not really in the equation, for now at least. We had the uncharted waters of Outer Mongolia to navigate yet.

It was astonishing to me that the Great Wall could have been built 2500 years ago, when the so-called "civilised" countries like America and Canada and even Britain were mere millennia away from their present, likely short-lived pinnacle of global domination. The fortunes of counties were after all cyclical. In another thousand years there might be a little boy in China asking what had become of the Olde Worlde Country of Englande. People now make a great show of immersing themselves in the Art of Chinese Medicine or Chinese philosophy or Geomancy, as if its all hip and new-fangled. They seem to forget that acupuncture has been around for more millennia than laser surgery has years, or that herbs were used in China for thousands of years before paracetamol and aspirin were officially invented!

There was a beautiful on-top-of-the-world serenity to the greenness that opened out before us, and the light morning breeze that surely carried pollen to us from the plains of Mongolia. This gentle reverie was interrupted only by the curious site of a camel carrying an assortment of Japanese tourists along the highest part of the wall. They were having the greatest difficulty holding their video cameras still which caused us much general merriment. We imagined all their friends back home, seasick now as well as bored, bobbing up and down to the sway of a camel's hips as they watched endless reruns of Mr Takahashi's Great Wall video.

LOOK CLOSELY,
ITS DEFINITELY A VEGETABLE!

That night we dined at a vegetarian restaurant that ironically boasted such carnivorous sounding dishes as "Peacock's Pride", "Devils scaling the peaks of the singing mountains" and assorted dog, chicken and beef delicacies. When questioned, the waiter did not understand our confusion. "But look", he gestured emphatically, rapidly losing patience. "Vegetables....". Oh yes, we said, understanding now. A vegetarian restaurant in China sold meat dishes with vegetables. We sat with an Italian couple whose names we never did get quite right despite lots of spitting and flaring of nostrils. He was quite fanatical about Persian carpets and Ming furniture, which must be a frustrating hobby to satisfy in rural Tuscany. His other obsession (his girlfriend, we assumed, was fourth on the list) was Tai Chi. He described with great pride how 152 Italians were coming to China the next week to attend an international symposium entitled Tai Chi for the 1990s. We tried to stay calm but the idea was frightening. Fortunately Laura did a quick calculation on the back of a beer mat and worked out we'd be safely tucked away in Outer Mongolia by the time the plane landed.

When we were done with dinner, Raf, for that's the closest we could get to his name, insisted on taking us to view a display of tai-chi outside the Temple of Heaven. It was quite magical, a concentrated mingling of mind and body that seems to completely absorb its participants. Except Raf, who talked loudly about the importance of inner calm throughout the whole ordeal. Some people held fans or swords in their hands as they moved with the utmost precision and in absolute unity through the hypnotic moves that focus the body's energy through carefully sculpted channels. Watching it had a soporific effect on us, we were quite entranced. I was amazed when it finished to see people just collapse to the ground, unable to walk, despite having executed such controlled and beautiful movements for almost two hours. It reinforced my original and here-to unshaken conviction that exercise, however innocently packaged, is invariably bad for you.

PETER USTINOV TELLS US ABOUT
A SMALL STONE MAN RIDING A CHICKEN

The next morning we awoke to find seven Lebanese men in oversized Y-fronts scurrying around our room. They had apparently lost a small cockatoo that they were taking home for their mother. The prodigious creator of these burly offspring apparently could not be allowed to die without seeing a small green Chinese budgie. Much as we sympathised in theory with their predicament, it was little after 6.00 am on a morning we'd allocated to lying in. The images of Y-fronts that persisted on our retinas were not conducive to sleep so we resigned ourselves to getting up.

Today we were going to be real, unashamed tourists and visit the Forbidden City, Imperial Home of the Manchus, including the Empress Wu Cixi, the son she'd allegedly kept under house arrest for the last years of his life and her grandson the ill-fated Last Emperor. I was excited to see where Peter O'Toole had slept but Laura reminded me that the Bernardo Bertolluci's Last Emperor had just been a film. I was marginally pacified to find the soft voice of Peter Ustinov, a man for whom I have always burnt a bit of a torch, crooning into my ears through the luxury in-house entertainment package (a 1970's walkman and a small black-and-white map). Having queued up at the foreigner's gate to pay our foreigners admittance fee in our foreigner's money, we filed under the unfeasibly large portrait of Chairman Mao that guarded the gates into the first main courtyard. The corner of Tiananmen Square flanking the entrance booth was scattered with multi-coloured fairground parasols shielding the purveyors of carbonated beverages and strange yellow corn bread from the morning drizzle.

It was incredibly busy, a huge number of Chinese as well as foreign tourists had piled through the austere gates of this legend-steeped, mysterious palace, off limits for 500 years to the mere mortals of the Chinese world. What must it have symbolised to the myriad beggars and peasants and families who worked outside its towering plum and mango walls in the scrawny grey stone cottages that flanked the moat. It was gratifying to find that even Peter Ustinov couldn't say with conviction what power these walls would have commanded. Amid the crushing poverty that festered on, unbridled in Beijing's slums, the Palace must have seemed as out of place as some Alien Empire would now, descending from the Clouds to squat on some majestic neon-rimmed throne in the clouds over Blackpool.

Unfortunately Laura and I were umbilically attached at the waist, having just one Peter and two pairs of headphones, and a succession of small old ladies and skipping children met an ugly fate half-garrotted on the wires of our luxury entertainment system. We tried to go around back to back, moving slowly in neat circles so as not to trip anyone up. Huddled in magnificent courtyards, laced with huge carved marble lozenges like slabs of finely veined cheese and with majestic bronze lions guarding the steps where emperors once climbed, stiff-backed, to the throne rooms and court halls. These rooms were other-worldly, the gold-screened throne with its fading silk cushions guarded by elaborate bronze incense holders on a platform with curved steps like bridges leading down to the black marble floor. Huge gold pillars, which started their life as trees brought in from three thousand miles away emblazoned with yellow-gold dragons soared up to the green, red and dragon-decorated ceiling, where the huge painted crossbeams sliced the ceiling into pencils of colour. The sheer vastness of the room was stunning, the coldness of the black marble floor where the economy-class courtiers would have stood. A similar, but smaller gate had red pillars, which peter Ustinov kindly informed us were tree trunks coated with a lacquer of pigs blood, tongue oil and musk. Not a decorating trend that would make a comeback in the near future, I suspected.

The courtyards were vast deserts of marble, blinding white against the mellow plum and mango of the roofs, each roof guarded against lightning (fire of course being a significant threat in a world built from wood and defended only by eunuchs) by a series of mystical roof creatures stationed along the roof-beams and led by a man on a chicken. Why? Not even Peter Ustinov could answer that one. Personally I would have thought a few whimsical stone animals and a man on a chicken would have wielded little power in a thunderstorm but who am I to comment. Apparently the Court used to contain many elephants, gifts from grovelling overseas ambassadors, and they were highly prized. If one of the Imperial elephants died, a period of mourning was declared. On a more practical note, elephant dung was discovered to have miraculous properties as a restorer of hair condition. I couldn't help wondering how they first discovered that one.

Laura was excited to find a man wandering around carrying a little leather pouch. With this interminable thing for eunuchs, she hoped to have found a pensioned off former retainer of the Imperial Court carrying his balls in a bag. Apparently eunuchs believed that when you departed to the next life you needed to be physically complete. Therefore the carefully dislocated appendages were carried day and night in a small leather pouch so that in the event of a sudden death situation the bearer may be fully tackled up. Horrifically, fifty percent of those who went through the risky surgery died in the process, on an ugly wooden chair with a strategically placed cut out section for ease of access to a gentleman's nether areas.

Half way through our tour, the Imperial Heavens opened and Peter started to get a little crackly. Just as we hunted round for a plastic bag to wrap him in, we noticed that every other person in the Forbidden City had had the same idea. Except their motive was not the dehydration of Peter Ustinov but the preservation of a perm or a facial. Mothers plucked bin liners from their hand-bags and popped them almost casually over their children's heads. Laura and I held our breath as they painstakingly slit holes for the nose and eyes and mouth to poke through. A few small children had already turned quite green by the time the ventilation system was fully up and running. In all, the Forbidden City was too much to take in and despite Peter's dulcet overtures purring in our ears, we finished the tour punch drunk and highly over-stimulated.

OUR TRAIN LEAVES WHEN????

We decided to commemorate our last night in Beijing with a trip to the Beijing Opera. It sounded romantic in a concubine-and-courtier kind of way and we pictured ourselves decked in diamonds and velvet (or new popsocs, our metaphorical equivalent) supping elegant vintage wines and peeping through opera glasses with critical, yet approving scrutiny at beautifully costumed actors from our exclusive box seats. Instead we found ourselves sharing a small drinks table with a party of Sichuanese book-binders. The general noise, aside from the Operatics, was ear-gratingly raucous as people traded jokes and hawked-up bodily products over our heads. Meanwhile the actors cavorted through the throws of opera with the movements of a 17th century breakdancer, writhing and twisting and doing a funny kind of moon-walk when things got particularly steamy on stage. It was the sound that would come to haunt us, high-pitched and wavering. I imagined it must take a very highly trained ear to appreciate the subtle differences in intonation and their inextricable significance to the unfolding of the plot. Given two years and a lot more tea, I wondered if we'd get there.

It might have been easier to follow the general story-line if the audience hadn't been busy creating a kind of generalised pandemonium apparently focusing on something someone had found in their teapot. Each table had a big pot of tea which was consumed with much general slurping and a lot of malodorous burping throughout the show. Now lots of people were gesticulating wildly and shouting at the waitresses. The show all but stopped as the actors tried to figure out what was going on. Fortunately they were peculiarly skilful in making surreptitious eye-movements which scared some of the small children and Scandinavian tourists in the front row, thereby creating a strategic diversion.

We outsat every other person at our table. Deeply committed to the cause of cross-cultural fertilisation we drank three pots of a curiously bland tea and tried hard to work out was going on. Sadly, it seemed that the meaning of the story hinged upon the actors' timely deployment of their ocular muscles: we didn't stand a chance. After two long hours in which our ears experienced the full range of audible frequencies, there was no sign of the plot being brought to any kind of logical conclusion so we made our excuses and left. Despite our confusion and the conflicting auditory information that bombarded us from all sides, the Opera had been beautiful. The costumes and backdrops and visual aesthetics had all been quite exquisite. We'd heard how during the Cultural Revolution, indeed, up to ten years ago, all of the old Operas, some of which went back hundreds of years, had been banned and only Operas which exhorted the selfless spirit of the die-hard revolutionary were allowed to be staged. Ironically many of the Operas had been written by Mao's wife, Jiang Qing, who would be sentenced to death (later commuted to life imprisonment) after Mao's demise for counter-revolutionary crimes against the State.

Determined to eat that night, despite the loss of a large portion of my Yuan, we headed off to find a restaurant called DongBinLou, specialising in Mongolian Hotpot (the shape of things to come) and Muslim barbecue, along with the ubiquitous Peking Duck. I suspected that some Peking Chickens were actually masquerading as ducks. Unfortunately we were too assertive in haggling with the taxi driver (we wanted him to take us there for 10 Yuan) so he drove at a snail's pace by way of protest, which meant we arrived just as they were closing the doors. It took most of our female charm just to get us in. Across the table from our dried out Chicken-Ghanzu dish and well-stewed broth of assorted duck entrails (including lungs, stomach and brains - by now we welcomed an innocuous little gizzard!) sat a family with a beautiful watchful baby. China's babies are something of an enigma. Invariably docile, expressionless, silent and apparently toilet-trained from birth, they seem to take everything in through their wondering, watchful eyes. They squat in the streets, balance nappyless on bicycle crossbars and behave better in restaurants than most adults I know. It seemed almost as if China's one family- one baby policy had somehow eradicated the all-dominant tantrum gene. Certainly the grabbing arrogance most infants seem to have in the West seems tempered in Chinese babies to a benign and irresistible cuteness. I felt unsettling stirrings in my ovaries for all the time we were in China.

We returned to the Qiaoyuan hotel (we were staying there that night to minimise the things that could possibly go wrong before morning) to begin packing at a leisurely pace for our big trip. The train left the following day at five in the evening and we desperately needed to stock up in the morning on provisions like toilet paper and tasty snacks. As we drizzled back into the lobby, weary from so much walking and Peter Ustinov all in one day, we bumped into Lou. With his usual smugness he reminded us to come up and fetch our passports. "Don't worry" called back Laura, in a cheery voice, "We'll pick them up tomorrow". "What point tomorrow exactly" demanded Lou with his usual tight-lipped sneer. There is a challenging note in his tone which we are quick to pick up on "Oh" answers Laura, with forced casualness. "Around three?". Lou, and all his sycophantic French-Canadian companions share a communal chuckle that sounds like a gurgling drain. "When were you thinking of catching the train?". "Five o'clock" answers Laura defiantly, getting into the swing of things. Secretly I think she is trying to impress this miserable git. "The train goes at five in the morning" he declares, triumphantly, waiting to see us cry. "We knew that" we trumpet back shakily, wobbling back into our room without a shred of dignity intact. So our train left in seven hours. We had no toilet paper, no delicious snacks and no instant coffee. It promised to be a very long trip indeed. While Laura scurried around the hotel stealing toilet paper from all the dormitories, I climbed back into my shoes and trundled back into the streets to find some provisions. Through various devious black-market means I managed to procure seven pot noodles, a small jar of Nescafe (it had some suspicious green bits in it), some ill-fated oranges that would meet a grisly fate under a fat Texan bottom just eight hours later, some toilet soap, a packet of crusty-looking lemon thins and a sad looking block of reconstituted goat's milk chocolate that smelled rancid even through three layers of tin foil. Fortunately we had high hopes for the buffet car which promised an exotic multi-cultural extravaganza of oriental culinary expertise or something like that. (It was hard to understand Lou when he started sneering).

China had been an amazing adventure for us. The people we'd met had been nothing but welcoming, despite the risks that we knew still shadowed them, even today. The maniacal, pet-slaying, sword-wielding robots we'd expected to find had never come out of the shadows. Our first thoughts in Canton were that grey, not red should be the colour associated with communism. But now, when we thought back on our time in China, we thought of it as red, not the Bolshevik red of Lenin and Mao but the warm red of friendship and hospitality and welcome and life. It had crept up on us suddenly, from Canton when the people seemed to menace and persecute us with their endless staring to Beijing where we jolted a man from sleep and he all but saved our lives.

We fell asleep that night reluctantly, waking every ten minutes to check that the alarm clock was still ticking and that the sky outside the window was still dark. It was about 4.45 am when we finally fell into a fitful sleep that was rudely terminated fifteen minutes later by the maniacal belching of Laura's alarm clock. We hadn't missed our train.

HOW WE WON
THE WAR WITH A POTTERY HORSE

About ninety kilometres out of Beijing and the scenery had already changed so much, carving through huge groves of willowy poplars and valleys of sunflowers bursting with yellow cheer. On the horizon to the north the thin grey bulk of the mountains blends with the sea-coloured sky. Already we felt that we were miles from anywhere. Our two new travelling companions had overly long legs that seem to dangle everywhere. They cast a wistful glance every now and again into the next carriage where people seemed to be having fun. Perhaps they expected us to be partying but we wanted to watch the world go by.

The clamour for compartments had been predictably frenetic, despite the reservations we all clutched in our greasy little paws which assured us of our right to board and be berthed. A slumbering paranoia seems to be awoken in the most sedate of us when space is small and time is tight. We found our compartment half-way down the carriage, already more than occupied by two disproportionately long Americans. Malcolm, a sad-looking chap from Oklahoma with a terminally melancholy disposition and an uncannily equestrian profile with his long face and strange forelock was groaning about an unfortunate experience with a Thai stir-fry the previous night. There was no need for him to tell us. He dolefully explained that he was something in stocks and shares and we commiserated respectfully. Whatever career path he had erroneously opted for, our limpid "mmmmm, we're still deciding what we want to do with our lives" (we were quite prickly about sounding like overgrown students) blurb sounded nothing short of spineless. While I blustered something cheesy about working with animals and small children, Russ, Malcolm's Texan friend, stifled a sarcastic scowl and went back to chewing his way through a packet of dried banana slices.

A solid looking woman in a heavy black dress drifted in after a couple of hours (she looked like how a friend of ours described any one of his wife's Eighteen Catholic Aunts) and swept all the fluff that had moulted from my bedroll into the corridor. A second, uncannily identical woman then swept the fluff along the corridor to a third identical lady who shunted it into the bathroom. This was communist job creation at its pinnacle of resourcefulness. We had seen this "one person one responsibility" system at work in China. The very idea of Job-Share was sufficient to bring most Chinese people out in metaphorical blisters. Accountability was everything and stepping a millimetre outside the confines of one's job description could open a minefield of pitfalls, snares, and, not surprisingly, mines. Apart from our experience trying to return our bicycles, we'd once tried to buy a postcard from a Chinese post- office to find that the person in charge of postcard sales was away, besides which we needed another person who was specifically in charge of postcard sales to Foreigners, but she was away having apparently some kind of accident involving chickens and was not expected back until 2004. The five other, apparently unoccupied sales people could not, therefore, sell us any postcards.

EXCUSE ME, I REALLY NEED TO ...

Restless and keen to explore our new airspace, I sauntered off into the corridor with the express intention of test-driving the bathroom. All that running for the train had precipitated a potential watershed. Just as I reached the door, one of the Sturdy Black Trinity appeared from nowhere to bar my way with a broom fashioned from pure steel. "Nyet" she scowled, eyeing me up and down with a frown. She held out her hand. Touched by this gesture of comradely warmth I reached out and shook her hand. She snapped away her hand and walked away shaking her head. The toilet door remained firmly locked.

Russ, a cooler, more upbeat breed of American with a slightly cocky but generally bearable edge to him refused to be told when to goddam urinate by an old Siberian lady with a broom. I took my metaphorical hat off to him as he crunched out into the corridor in overly tight jeans to shift some Siberian butt. We waited in silence punctuated only by Malcolm's periodic flatulent outbursts. Sure enough, just two minutes later, Russ came back, cross-legged and slightly flushed. He kicked the door like they do in the movies. I'm sure it must have hurt his foot. Just then an elderly Chinese man with a rattling trolley laden with cardboard boxes clattered noisily past our compartment and the veins on Russ's head started to pulse. I sensed he Russ was teetering on a delicate neural tightrope and feared for our safety in this tiny little cabin.

Malcolm then wandered off, amiably lollopy with his long neck and bendy ankles. From our compartment we hear only the thin squeak of his little detonation, then the clamour of keys scrabbling for the lock. While he would later claim in a show of bravado that he had smoked her out, we knew he'd slipped her a couple of Marlborough cigarettes. Our hands were tied. Malcolm alone had the unofficial key to urinary liberation. While the rest of us deliberated over the potential usefulness of a pot noodle container in an urgent toilet situation, Malcolm popped off at his convenience to detonate in the relative privacy of his own little cubicle.

By the end of the afternoon Laura and I had raided our backpacks and come up with a packet of nylons, two chocolate bars, three Bic biros, two bars of toilet soap, a slightly soggy postcard showing Peter Ustinov astride some sort of gazelle, an English guide to the Forbidden City, a cast iron wastepaper basket and a small pottery horse. We laid them out on our bed while Russ and Malcolm went prowling for talent in the adjacent cubicles, and called in two of the identical women who patrolled the toilet. The older lady seemed very taken with the little pottery horse, petting him and stroking him and generally seeming very grateful. The other one, despite our firmest offers, declined to take the cast iron wastepaper basket and opted for the nylons, toilet soap and the photograph of Peter Ustinov. With a nod and a wink they bid us follow them at a distance down the corridor where three quick coughs would signify the unofficial de-cloaking of the bathroom door . All this was conveyed through hand gestures and lots of hushed whispers that we couldn't understand.

Once I got in there, I was determined not to be too quick in case this was the only time we could get in, so I stopped and had a good look around while I waited for any additional flow to accumulate. Stacked all around the back of the toilet were case upon case of Chinese vodka, mostly unopened. Evidently this was what they'd been carrying on those interminable trolleys that kept rattling past our compartment. From the cupboard under the sink something furry protruded. I was sure I saw it move and approached it with due trepidation. Closer investigation revealed a stash of fur coats, screwed up in a plastic bin liner and stashed under the leaky U-bend. Raised on a Sunday afternoon diet of Hercule Poirot and Miss Marples, I immediately sensed that something was amiss.

Malcolm had an explanation for this, as he did for most things. It seemed that many of the Chinese passengers legitimately or illegitimately travelling on the train were engaged in dodgy import-export scams, shipping furs, drinks, western cosmetics and brand-name sportswear across the border into Mongolia and thereon into Russia. Precision handling of the various carriage attendants, lubricated where possible by hard western currency, was imperative to ensure that immigration officials were detained elsewhere during the customs inspection, to the unwelcome surprise of say, a small man from Prague who might find himself tossed out of bed in the middle of the night. Also fundamental to the scheme was a safe place for storage of the illicit goods during the customs inspection. Which was where we came in. Lou had told us that all foreigners were incarcerated together in a separate carriage, purportedly for our own protection. (Given the fluctuating mental state of our present bedfellow, there was a certain irony to the notion that we'd all form one big pasty-skinned huddle and menace all the bad people with our phoney English accents). But now it seemed more likely that our carriage offered handy storage space for illegal merchandise while we crossed the Chinese border. Immigration officials, we later found out, were unlikely to search foreigners' compartments because they disliked our general eggy smell. This from a Russian car-mechanic who had yet to meet Malcolm.

NEVER, NEVER EAT
AN INNER MONGOLIAN WATER MELON

Sometime that evening, having secured unlimited toilet privileges and spent many happy hours urinating in white-enamel comfort, the train stopped at a small Chinese border town. We didn't see much of the town, but if the quality of a neighbourhood is judged by the atmosphere of conviviality in its drinking houses, there was probably little to see. We poured into a bar, fifty of us in various stages of deteriorating personal hygiene. The bar was plastered in an unforgettable floor to ceiling psychedelic orange vinyl, strangely bohemian given the tepid German waltzes that dribbled from the one speaker. The walls were shrouded in a net of glittering Christmas fairy lights that themselves were shadowed into oblivion by the soporific spinning of the largest disco ball I had ever seen. I wondered if the Russians knew that a vital part of their space armament was beached here on the Outer Mongolian border.

Just then Mr Takahashi, who seemed to think his first class berth entitled him to more than truly clean sheets and a slightly larger facecloth, erupted in a paroxysm of excitement. It was the first time we'd seem he achieve even amoebic heights of animation and the guards, who had been watching us all with disinterested suspicion, were quick to put their hands on their guns. He'd found a karaoke machine. This curiously addictive entertainment concept originated in Japan to give frustrated Japanese businessmen the chance to croon vulgar western words at the ladies in their office in the cause of art. Shortly after the advent of karaoke, Air Thailand reduced the cost of weekend flights to Thailand which further helped liberate those hot-blooded males from the shackles of sexual repression. By now Mr Takahashi had clambered across the dance-floor and was almost rubbing up against the microphone. We watched in some amazement. The first image that flickered onto the karaoke screen knocked me just about off my socks. There, on the screen, was a tiny rural Japanese village with a population of no more than 3,000 people, cows and strangely snub-nosed dogs. It was the village I had just left behind, and there, sliding now into view on the right, was the little apartment block where I'd lived for two years. I could almost see Mrs Ubara in the flat above pinning out her laundry in the window. It was unexpectedly nostalgic and strangely aroused in me the sudden urge to urinate.

Unfortunately the toilets were locked, but two smiling ladies with beautiful red cheeks ushered me conspiratorially into the men's toilets, promising to keep a watchful guard. At least I think that's what they were promising. All seemed well until the door closed and the room was cast into complete and utter darkness. Wary of stroking an unfamiliar men's urinal I edged my way across the floor. Something sloshed over the top of my flip-flop. Don't think about it, don't think about it, I repeated to myself like a mantra, scouting that foot further and further forward. At the very moment I became aware of a kind of asthmatic rasping right in front of me my foot sank into something squodgy. There was a man, sitting on the toilet, right there in front of me. He grunted and I squeaked like a helium balloon. With a gung-ho disregard for the finer points of hygiene I groped my way along the sticky wall back to the door and burst back out into the hallway panting like a cheetah. As I came out, one of the customs officials went in. It still seemed pretty dark in there but he obviously knew his way around. He emerged two minutes later carrying a very ripe pair of watermelons. I resolved at that point never to eat an Inner Mongolian watermelon.

WHAT DO YOU MEAN, YOU DON'T SPEAK MONGOLIAN?

The tracks at this point changed from the Chinese gauge to the Russian gauge which was three and a quarter inches narrower. The Chinese engine had to be taken off the front of the train and replaced by its Russian counterpart, an innocent enough manoeuvre grimly described as "changing the bogies". Led back onto the train eventually at 12.14 a.m. we drifted into an uneasy sleep that featured too many men with watermelons. But somewhere around 1.30 o'clock we were plucked from sleep by the incessant battering of a what sounded like a gun on our compartment door and an unearthly screaming sound. Fearing this might just tip Russ over the edge, I tried to reassure him its all just a dream but it was too late, he was all wild-eyed and foaming mouthed. Outside our door stood two Mongolian officials in their full regalia complete with gold epaulettes and interesting tassel-formations on their hats. One of them, a lady in a chilling shade of iced-raspberry lipstick and some pretty impressive eye-make-up started prodding us with the but of her gun while burbling unintelligibly in Mongolian.

A form was thrust in front of us, written entirely in a language we couldn't begin to understand. There were twenty-five categories or questions, each neatly staked on in its own little box. We could only fill in two of them, our name and age, before adding our signatures at the bottom of the page. The lady stabbed crossly with the but of her gun at category 14 and made a generous hand gesture that suggested water-melons. I wondered what possible criminal convictions involving water-melons we were expected to confess to. The shock, meanwhile, had not proved good for Malcolm's bladder. The shock of finding the toilet was locked and would not be open again until "morning", a fairly imprecise term given that it was now 2.30 am, proved even harder. While she prodded him in the belly and drew his attention to item 17 which seemed to involve animals, he groaned and doubled up in pain. In retrospect what happened next was inevitable. Malcolm ushered us out of the compartment. We knew what would happen next and didn't want to be around to see it. We had all discussed how, if times got really desperate, we'd have to use the pot noodle container. A man had to do what a man had to do.

Unfortunately however, poor Laura just hadn't got out in time. Mired on the top bunk on a strangely slippery mattress (a sudden movement could send her skidding onto the floor) she was busy calculating her best motor trajectory when Malcolm gave the evacuation orders. We can only guess at what the poor girl must have seen. To make things even more uncomfortable, the door then locked itself magically from the inside and the best endeavours of Laura, Malcolm, Russ, myself and the two Mongolian immigration officials could not dislodge the catch. Eventually a Russian car mechanic was called in from the next compartment to release the mechanism. He was quite a versatile guy. Back in bed eventually, at 3.00 o'clock, we all slipped into a dreamless sleep.

I awoke early the next morning and felt the first warmth of light seeping in through the window. The horizon, uncannily flat, seemed to be bleeding pink and red and yellow into the black sky. Where yesterday the wind had combed Mongolia's prairies into neat bristling rows that tussled and jostled, there was now the blackest of blacks cowering under a violent sky. The Gobi Desert. I watched and watched as the skies stopped simmering and grew calmer, and the soft sands of the desert took shape from the blackness. The desert was not the alabaster kind, silky and white like talcum powder, but rough and endless, punctuated only by scattered rocks and boulders and the occasional grassy stump patrolled by packs of wolves. Falcons skimmed low over the rocks, grazing the sands with the tips of their wings. In the distance, camels, real camels, idled in the morning mists. I was quite excited to see my first camel and bellowed at some volume "camel ahoy". I knew they weren't really sleeping but not one of them could be bothered to look out the window!

THANKS, I'LL HAVE THE BEETROOT

Hungry from the night's adventures and out of lemon thins, Laura and I decided with misplaced excitement to brave the dining car. A lady in a splendid green velvet evening gown resembling Finland's national dress and a full battery of diamante accessories welcomed us to our seats and gave us a menu bound in red satin and held together with a tatty gold tassel. Excited to see the delicious menu items on offer, we plumped for two tomato soups and a roast chicken dinner. The word "menu" in Mongolian is apparently derived from the root "fiction". Today for example, despite the stunning array of international cuisine on offer in the menu, we could have either Borsch, a curiously vinegary beetroot product or Beef Stroganoff. When questioned more closely she confessed that there was rather less beef than stroganoff in the beef stroganoff. And the borsch was all gone. So what was actually on offer was a generic stroganoff derivative that turned out to be some kind of cornflour and vodka paste presented with a strange yellow potato (just the one) that tasted of bleach and a small side-serving of assorted deep-fried cow offal.

While we chewed and chewed and chewed people around us traded cashmere sweaters and dubious methanolic spirits with hand-written labels. Behind them we watched the constantly shifting background unfold, wild horses cavorting in dancing throngs and fields of belligerent-looking sheep whipped into order by dashing Mongolian horsemen in magnificent orange robes. As we headed back to recover from breakfast, we met a man coming out of the toilet with an empty trolley, clutching a crispy green fistful of dollar notes. "Change money?" he offered with a winning smile. (We had developed quite a thing for these fiery eyed Mongolians with their flushed cheeks and beautiful teeth.) Given that foreigners were forbidden to possess, trade or use the Mongolian Tugrik, we wondered exactly what he had in mind. Fortunately we were distracted by a field of two-humped camels, all standing around, knocked kneed and despondent looking, facing different directions. They reminded me a little of Malcolm.

OUTER MONGOLIA

The scenery for that next leg of the trip was amazing, the undulating hills of northern China melting into the vast expanses of grass that characterise the flatlands of the Mongolian prairie. From our privileged train window vantage point we watched rural life unfold along the tracks that sliced through the landscape. Families loaded onto horse-drawn carts ploughed upstream churning up muddy river beds. People in mudbrick farming communes worked the paddies by hand, bent over nearly in half at the middle, children skittered out of dried-mud courtyards to wave at the train. Solitary goat herds steered flocks of one or two hundred goats across the grasslands that flanked the tracks. Barefooted children chased wild horses along the side of the train, the rush and roar of the horses hooves almost in time with the clattering of our metal wheels. The beauty was breathtaking, and in our minds all the people we saw were kissed by a warm wind which whipped their hair about their red cheeks and tore the words from their mouths as they hurtled past us. The sheer size and desolation of these endless grasslands was inconceivable to us, raised in the cut-throat urban pace of Milton Keynes and Manchester.

Eventually the grasslands gave way to a rougher, rockier landscape, which deteriorated into a vast concrete graveyards with slag heaps and endless rows of pylons and powerlines criss-crossing a vista of blackened factory roofs. Some of the installations looked derelict, half-overgrown with shrubs and grasses, rusted through or slowly sinking into the sands. Around the ruins children ran with brightly coloured kites while men on horses galloped towards the horizon on strangely short-legged ponies. Malcolm cheerfully assured us that this was Ulan Bator.

Despite the inauspicious approach to Ulan Bator, the hotel itself was an amazing creation, decked out in Mediterranean hues of primrose yellow and aquamarine blue with long purple, pink and orange rugs with elaborately woven borders running across the vivid orange vinyl floor. It felt more like a small Greek fishing harbour than the capital of Outer Mongolia. Given the greyness of Ulan Bator's industrial hinterland the psychotic vigour of these Van Gogh-esque colours was unexpected and revived our spirits and we hurried our way through lunch so we could set out to see the city.

Whatever our expectations had been, I think we would still have been surprised. Ulan Bator was a chocolate box of a town, whimsically cutesified by its pink and tangerine orange plasterwork and wedding cake alabaster frills skirting windows and roofs and doorways. My mouth watered to see its gingerbread houses and sponge-cake ministerial offices with their white-icing columns and stately, symmetrical squareness. Given the industrial gloom of the suburbs, this mischievous frivolity seemed absurd, knowing nothing at the time about Mongolia's history or traditions. It seemed a city all set for assemblies in the wide concrete plazas, for picnics in the public parks, for sun-kissed lovers strolling through the empty boulevards. Instead couples cavorted on the back seats of pre-war Skodas or trucks fashioned from sheets of tin metal bolted together, wrestling with the practicalities of the knee length leather boots and the magnificent velvet padded coats worn by all the men. Russ, being a good Texan boy, was quite upset to see what he called "men in skirts". Almost all the people we saw were wearing shades, an unnecessary precaution given the interminable drizzle that day, and grey felt hats pulled down over the eyes and tipped jauntily to one side which gave them all the air of 1960's gangsters

We were amazed by the large number of children and young people in the streets and in the innumerable concrete playgrounds with their invariable complement of concrete zoo animals. An old man selling elastic bands in a department store would later explain that people either got out young or died early. Our initial whimsical impression of Ulan Bator as a pleasure palace for the young and restless was popped. He suggested we think of it more like a large pink waiting room.

It was a little denting to our egos to be so conspicuously ignored. In Japan, Hong Kong and China our body fat and frizzy curls commanded almost celebrity status. Here people seemed hostile, sinister even, watching us guardedly or not at all. The only people who consistently acknowledged our existence were the tour-guide (it was illegal to enter Outer Mongolia at this time without being in the nominal custody of an "official" tour-guide) and the hotel porter who asked us every time we saw him whether we wanted to exchange our valuable US dollars for the useless, illegal Mongolian Tugrik.

SORRY, FREDDIE MERCURY MUGGED US JUST FIVE MINUTES AGO...

Our friendly tour guide advised us over dinner, without a hint of irony, that it was customary (he made it sound like an ancient cultural ritual) for local Mongolian men to go out at night to drink, get boisterous and have a few knife fights. He made it seem like the wild wild west with swashbuckling gangsters mobbing stagecoaches and making young ladies in corsets swoon so we poo-pooed his advice with a "I think we know what we're doing" kind of smugness, determined to experience Mongolia at night. Our mistake. ﹒

Leaving a fairly sad Mongolian bar at around eleven o'clock, we (being Laura, myself, an Irish girl called Miranda and Mr Takahashi) set a fast pace home through the dimly-lit back streets. As we rounded the corner, a group of Mongolian men sprang almost from nowhere, swaying with alcohol as they staggered to block our path. The tallest one lunged at me, grabbing me by my hair and pinning me to the ground. I tried to blind him with my dairy smell but he seemed strangely resistant. His fingers dug in deeper and deeper. I knew I had a whistle stashed in one of my pockets but I couldn't reach it so I squealed in what I imagined was a "whistle"- ish way. It gave him quite a fright and bought me a few valuable seconds but lacking any presence of mind I frittered them away in a quagmire of panic. Laura, Miranda and Mr Takahashi had by now rounded on him, as well as his two friends, and were trying to pry his fingers out of my hair which was not the most comfortable thing for me. I screamed for Laura to get my wallet from my pocket. In it I knew he would find one US dollar, the rest of my money being stashed away in a money belt against my belly. It was a precaution we'd made almost laughingly as we'd got ready to go our. She gave him the purse and he loosened his hold. Theoretically it was the best offer I'd had in the whole of our travels.

All but hysterical by now but strangely elated by our brush with the Mongolian underworld we scurried round a corner into the hands of a man with a unfeasibly well-groomed moustache and large hunkering biceps (I don't think the two were connected) who was ranting deliriously about Mongolia and the motherland. We tried to turn around but he grabbed me, almost breaking Miranda's hand as she reached out to stop him and wrestled me to the ground. One of his friends materialised as if from nowhere and pinned Mr Takahashi against a post like they do in the movies with his feet dangling in mid-air. Three other friends bullied us out the way with rough cuffs as we tried to come forward to rescue him. At one point we all broke free and sped off across a field, but they caught up with us again and began kicking us to the ground. I scraped my nails down the back of the man with the moustache (actually he looked a bit like Freddie Mercury) and Laura bit the finger of a man in dark glasses. Grabbing for my whistle, which I'd been carrying around for four weeks and never had occasion to use, I noticed the men all turn and stare. I held it out " you want?" I cried defiantly, backing away. They walked slowly after us with a just-got-off-me-horse waddle as I baited them with the whistle. We were all out of their immediate reach now, and with a final scream we flung the whistle at them and bolted for our hotel across a field. Unfortunately we had failed to take into account the fact that we were lost and ended up running at least two miles around the town, screaming loudly before running round any corners to scare off any potential assailants. One stoned looking man sitting under a tree raised his arm as we ran past so we threw him a wallet just to be sure. Just after that, we recognised the familiar heating vent at the back of our hotel and heltered across the playground to the relative sanctuary of our Mediterranean oasis. Or so we thought. Inconvenienced by our dual muggings and therefore running slightly late, the porter had gone off to bed leaving the door locked and a picture of a clock showing the sun coming up. We hammered and hammered on the door, breathless now and on the verge of hysteria as we pictured the mad Mongols raging down on us through the playground, scimitars glinting in the moonlight.

We hammered and hammered some more, until the porter eventually could be seen making his deliberately ponderous way across the orange vinyl floor. Opening the door just a smidgen, he asked "change money?" through the crack. Impotent and hysterical, we gave him the last of our little plastic wallets. Enough adventure for one day.

THERE ARE MANY WAYS TO COOK LIVER

In the cold light of morning the precious night's events receded to a bizarre and rather exotic memory with a lot of potential mileage for scaring our parents and making us sound brave. We congratulated ourselves on our bravado and resourcefulness, both already embellished in our imagination to superhero proportions. I would also come to mourn the loss of my whistle, but we agreed he'd been brave to the end and dedicated a fleeting moment to his tinny little memory over a breakfast of carrot and rice omelette and pancake bread. Still, there was definitely a taste of something other than Freddie Mercury's aftershave left in our mouths and we approached Ulan Bator the next morning with a slightly less rose-tinted view. Our tour-guide certainly was impressed to see us hanging on his every word for the rest of the trip.

Breakfast featured the ubiquitous goat meat and carrot combination and we shared it with an Inner Mongolian lady who spoke fluent English. We confessed our naiveté of the previous night to her. "This happens a lot", she said. "Since the Russians pulled out of here a couple of years ago, the machinery and industry has gone to pot. Food processing, textiles, fertiliser production were all Mongolian industries but now no-one can fix the machinery so people cannot work. There is very little money here. So all the men drink cheap import vodka at night and look for fights so they take it out on someone. It's very sad." Somehow this seemed to put things in more perspective for us. It was not as much as personal attack as an expression of the dissatisfaction of the country as a whole. It also explained all the decaying machinery scattered on the outskirts of the city like some half-abandoned carcass in an advanced stage of dismemberment. By way of afterthought she added "But its true that the Mongols can't stand the Japanese. They look almost the same but have so much more money. It's hard to take".

That morning we headed off to see the Mongolian state department store, which waited hesitantly in the middle of a street overgrown with weeds and patrolled by a surly looking herd of spotted cows. It had six stories, and was a true wedding cake of a store. Near the entrance door as we went in was a sign outlining the merchandise available on each storey, from women's lingerie on floor two to hunting rifles on floor six. Inside it was flashily decked out with mirrored ceilings and elaborate enamel counter-tops and incredible marble pillars. Almost the whole store was empty. All we could find was a small counter on the second floor selling yo-yos, Halloween masks, leather riding boots, tiny wooden puzzles selling for 0.04 pence, spring onions and small bundles of elastic bands, as well as long out-of-date mars bars at $1 a piece.

Hungry now after our feast of carrots forty minutes earlier, we headed to the Department Store Bakery where the guide book promised us "a mouth-watering selection of cakes and cookies and breads". Maybe, but not today. A small carton of green tomatoes and some dehydrated onion flakes were all we could find for sale. Just then a lorry backed up into the docking area at the back of the store, and started unloading crate upon crate upon crate into the loading bay. Local people swarmed over from each end of the main town square, clamouring to see what was in the boxes. The delivery guy then leapt into the tray, and we could see scraps of some burnt rusk-like biscuits all around his leather boots. People started wailing as he scooped the rusks out of the crates into bags that people held out to him. Apparently this was the weekly bread delivery from Mongolia's only bakery.

Apparently the food crisis had become much more severe since the Democratic Revolution three years earlier, when the Russians had left. We just couldn't understand where people got their food from. Even when the bread came in, there was no guarantee you'd get any. It was the usual Mongolian system of payment - you queued up for a long time at one counter to pay then took your receipt to the man in the crates to get the bread if there was any left. Plus you could only buy bread if a) - you were Mongolian and b) - you had your own shopping bag, because the man emptied the bread straight into the bag. We failed to score on both accounts. It was irrelevant however because we could not in all conscience begin to try and stake a claim to any of these rations that, for all we knew, could have to last months. We had the certainty of our imminent return to Western supermarket shopping at the end of our road, whereas these people had little certainty at this time for the future.

Today's lunch featured carrot surprise, the surprise being that it was carrot and little else. Carrot soup and carrot stew to be precise with a strange carroty orange bread product. There was also an usually wet meat dish in a vinegary sauce that sloshed around like cold liver on our plates. Unfortunately the restaurant was having another power cut, so the lights were low and it was difficult to see what we were eating but we battled away trying to slide the meat onto our forks in the darkness. We did wonder fleetingly why the curtains were closed, thereby excluding any hope of natural light penetrating our eating area, but thought little of it, enjoying the soporific calm of the vinegary half-light. It was only when a Swedish lady called Helga let forth a small cry that we all woke up. She had tweaked open the blind to facilitate accurate lipstick application and noticed that her meat dish was unusually red. Closer inspection revealed that the meat was actually a liverish product that seemed strangely untouched by any of the traditional cooking methods such as frying, boiling, steaming or roasting. We spluttered as we flushed morsels of apparently raw meat from between our teeth in the uncomfortable company of people we barely knew. For days afterwards the smell of vinegar would trigger a violent gag reflex in all those who had ever eaten at Chez Khan.

A TOURIST TRAIL OF MONGOLIAN CULTURE

It was stipulated on our visa documents (it could have said Mr and Mrs WooWoo and their seventeen poodles and we wouldn't have known any different) that we had to take a tour of Mongolian culture during our stay in Ulan Bator, so we resigned ourselves to a day on a tour bus. The bus was an unnecessary gesture as all the sights were within half a mile of each other. We started off with a visit to the State Museum, where we were treated to a fascinating display of the "Minerals of Mongolia". Thankfully this gave way to some interesting exhibits on wildlife and agriculture. Mongolia's fauna is breathtaking, reindeer (which are ridden in the west of Mongolia), snow leopards, vultures, bears, lynx cats, kangaroo rats, beavers, gazelles and huge spiders with a deadly looking red cross marked on their backs that can apparently kill with one bite. There was also a rather incongruous exhibition on dinosaurs, with huge fossilised dinosaur eggs, a Tyrannosaurus Rex skeleton and loads of teeth and bones. The Gobi desert had been the site of a major find in the dinosaur world a decade or so before and apparently somewhere on the fringes of the Gobi four large aerosol painted blue and red dinosaurs had been specially built from concrete to commemorate the find. In my mind I thought we saw them one morning from the train through the early morning mists but

Laura, ever the voice of reason, insists that I imagined the whole thing. Knowing my own imagination, I have to believe her.

In the afternoon we went to visit a monastery, a real functioning Lama monastery. It was indescribable from a visual point of view, a vibrant painting in reds, yellows and oranges, with monks in two flavours, the elderly or the prepubescent varieties, sporting vast orange and red robes and padding in huge riding boots with up-turned toes through the paved courtyards. With incredible dignity they managed to ignore us, (cringefully conspicuous as we were in our radioactive rain-gear) veer round moon-faced Mongolian children chasing pigeons and a strange red puppy, and carry on chanting. On one wall, thirty old men with the most fascinating faces, weathered and wise, leaned against the mango-coloured wall chatting. Other mere mortals in traditional dress pressed their heads against the temple buildings, stones, even telegraph poles and rubbed their hands over their faces and through their hair.

Inside the temples, a service was in full sway. The building itself was a dizzying kaleidoscope of colours, huge hanging wallcloths and pillars with bold fabric designs and the chicken-coloured monks' robes bright against the wooden chairs. Tiny boys of about five or six were in control of the drum and from time to time the monks' chanting, which trailed off to a tepid mumbling after ten minutes or so would be interrupted by a crash of cymbals which would wake the men and restore the full throttle of the chanting. The younger boys were alert and watchful, keeping an eye on everything and everyone, rubbing incense pearls in each others hair like monkeys, scratching each other's shoulders, fiddling with their prayer cards. I could have watched for hours, the atmosphere was quite soporific, with the smells of incense and gentle chanting like cicadas after the rains. It was humbling to be a part, however peripheral, of this service. We knew how during the communist crackdown of the 1930's about 14,000 monks were killed in the Ulan Bator area alone. This was the only one of seven hundred formerly functioning monasteries left in the Ulan Bator area. The monks really paid no attention to us. Rather we felt uncomfortable because they were in their space, their world and we were the intruders who didn't belong.

IS THERE A "G" IN GULLIBLE?

At the post-office we bought about five dollars worth of Mongolian post cards which all featured unusual artists' recreations of dinosaurs and two dollars worth of stamps. The stamps all featured drawings of alien spacecraft, a recurring theme of conversation here, and were approximately 2 . 5 inches square, which left very little room to actually write anything. This was our kind of correspondence. Just as we were leaving the post office, a lady and a young ten or eleven year old girl who we took to be her daughter moved in step with us and began questioning us at length about Chinese immigration and the amount of hard western currency we thought it would take to get a Chinese visa. Cheerfully naive as ever and anxious to share stories of our various brushes with bureaucracy, we vented at length on the illogicality of international immigration policy. Then she asked us back to her house for tea, and to see a real Mongolian House. At first I thought she said horse, which would have been interesting given that she apparently lived in a fourth floor apartment. Ignoring our gut instinct and anxious to culturally assimilate we agreed that we'd visit tomorrow. She was quite persistent. Neither of us met the eye of the tour guide that night.

By the next morning we had rationalised that she would probably have forgotten about the whole thing and so made plans that co-incidentally avoided the post office and the whole quadrant of the city where she lived. With gay abandon then, we set off across the main platz towards the monastery - who should we she but the curiously persistent lady bearing down on us with lots of waving and generally fevered animation. She knew, she said with a maternal chide, that we must have got lost, so she'd come looking for us. Chilling flashbacks from Fatal Attraction zipped through my mind. A little unnerved, but utterly gutless, we concurred with an "uuurrrrrrrrr" sound before following her through a maze of sponge-cake backstreets and up four flights of stairs. Still half-expecting to see a horse, I ducked slightly as we went through the door. The apartment was the most minty shade of green I have ever encountered and we instantly stifled a shiver. There was an elderly lady propped up on the sofa, whom she introduced as her mother. Before we could say "bring back our coats" and "where did you put our shoes?" we were looking at a tray neatly plastered in doilies laden with goats milk cheese and carrot sticks and two cups of buttery Mongolian tea. The atmosphere was crushingly awkward. Sure enough, just five minutes into the small talk about our home towns and family, she asked, point blank, if we'd be so kind as to change all our American dollars into Mongolian Tugriks at 30% of the going rate so that she could send her daughter to China. We sat in a dribbling and frozen state, feeling desperately awkward in her house, as her guest, declining to hand over our money and wondering how much that cheese had cost her. Besides, we explained, it was illegal for us to possess Tugriks. She dismissed that with an irritated "tut" and a flick of her hand. We listened politely but as she grew more persistent and the daughter's and grandmother's cries added to the chorus we stumbled to our feet and backed out at speed, still stepping into our shoes which we'd found behind the radiogram. Gratifyingly, our initial gut feeling warning us away from this lady was legitimised when, leaving her apartment, we met her daughter shepherding another big hairy westerner up the fire-escape. Given her grandmother's unquestioned acceptance of our intrusion into the family home and her nonchalant lack of interest in where we came from and what we were doing in Ulan Bator, we could conclude that visitations from foreigners were a fairly commonplace occurrence. Our indignation stemmed as much from irritation that our travellers tool of raw intuition had let us down and from that awareness of privilege that travellers wrongly describe as "guilt", as from a sense of having been tricked. We were disorientated too, in a way, without the disembodied collection agencies that took all responsibility and humanity out of charity with their neat sticky envelopes and anonymous collection boxes. You didn't have to put much thought into giving at all. But we had to judge what and who and where were most deserving and we couldn't begin to do it. I don't believe in the argument that because you can't do all things for all people you shouldn't so anything for anyone. But like most travellers, I suppose, we wanted to come, take a lot, give a little, then go.

KEEP HIM SWEET: HE'S THE ONLY ONE
WHO CAN GET US OUT OF HERE

We always seemed to travel on the same bus, or if we didn't, the bus driver somehow knew it and changed buses to be with us. He was an older man with a conspicuous absence of teeth and a sturdy walk. Every day he had taken to appearing in our room asking us to change money and twice had taken advantage of my dishevelled bleariness in the morning to plonk a fat wet kiss on my ears and on my nose. This morning he was booked to take us to the Bogha Khan Palace, which turned out to be indefinitely closed for repairs. By way of compensation we were swiftly re-routed to a small temple museum that displayed religious costumes and masks that had survived the 1930s crackdown on religious expression. Fifty of us poured out of the bus to the surprise of the bearded curator who looked a little overwhelmed. Through a crack in the wall behind the temple we watched the bus driver flag down unsuspecting members of the Mongolian public and, crumpling a crispy handful of notes into their palms lead them into a little ante-room at the back of the altar. He seemed fairly indiscriminate in his heckling, two semi-functional limbs and an approximate sense of standing balance seemed his only criteria. After about thirty minutes, a man in a mask came out and bowed gravely before us. There was a vaguely funereal sweep to his arm which would turn out to be strangely prophetic. Behind him came two men, the same men, no less, who had thirty minutes earlier been sent out by their wives to buy carrots, dressed one as a cow and one as some kind of wizard in long silk robes that swished the cigarette butts away from the temple gateway. They proceeded to cavort arthritically through the gyrations of what we were assured was an ancient religious dance but what we suspected was a kind of newly invented twirling. Twirling in its wobbliest sense. We wondered if they were trying to reach the ecstatic heights achieved in the swirling dervishes. If so this was going to take a very long time.

Just then the gentleman in the cow costume managed to wrap himself around a fifteenth century pillar not quite avoiding a confrontation with a generously proportioned American Lady in a very voluminous raincoat. He recovered quite well but was visibly shaky throughout the remainder of the performance. One of his horns remained slightly unhinged, not unlike the rest of us, for the remainder of the performance. The funereal little man who'd come out first was clanging two symbols together with a brave disregard for rhythm. The clanging seemed interminable. Eventually we all poured forward and offered a dollar each for them to stop. With the charitable glow of hindsight, we wondered if that had been their plan all along. Meanwhile the bus driver seemed disproportionately excited by my thigh length raincoat and started stroking his finger down the back of my neck. Before I could rap his knuckles, the doors of the temple burst open and we all took in a gasp of anticipation. I moved back towards the bus driver. If this was another madman disguised as a fifteenth century farm animal I might need to keep him in a good mood. It looked like he was the only one who could get us out.

But no, it was ten of our tour party who had become inextricably embroiled with a man they were calling The New Genghis Khan. He had menaced them with his swirling hand movements and all-weather rainboots for over thirty minutes in complete and utter darkness except for a small miner's helmet that he wore on his head. Authentically dressed for his role as Rain Warrior in five layers of fur, lots of leather hosiery and a very big drum (he looked a bit like Hiawatha), he contorted himself through the throws of some kind of other-worldly heavy-rock concert with lots of shouting and "ugh" sounds. One pleasant lady from Droitwich had to be taken away to lie down. Having made their break from the museum room, (a small German man called Jonathan apparently carried a small sprocket set in his pockets for just such emergencies), they gulped in the bright blue air. Genghis burst forth from the museum chamber and they all let forth a small scream and started scurrying for the bus. The bus-driver beckoned me over. "Please get us out" I whispered but he just tickled me behind the chin. Fortunately it all seemed very nearly over. Genghis was convulsing on the floor through what appeared to be the final throws of orgasm and the rain had nearly stopped. The symbols wound down to a thin clicking sound and the man in the cow costume had plucked a carrot from his trousers and sat down to eat.

We turned and started climbing onto the bus. Just as we were starting to pull away, Genghis Khan climbed onto the bus and accosted two of our party, Shaun, an outspoken Lancastrian and his Australian wife Kerry, demanding five dollars because they'd apparently taken a video film of his "art". As Shaun had been locked in the darkness of the museum hall during the display (he'd been too late to make a break for it with the others) this seemed a little cheeky. Nevertheless, Genghis was irate. Fluffing his fingers through his chicken-feather head-dress and banging very loudly on his drum he invoked the curse of Genghis Khan by shouting "Genghis Khan is comiiiiiiinnnnnngggg" at Shaun, Kerry and me. I don't think it was personal but I happened to be sitting next to them. In the next two hours we had black sausage for lunch, Shaun lost his lens cap and I developed a gippy stomach. Bloody Genghis Khan.

WHAT THE CHIEF OF THE MONGOLIAN NATURAL DISASTERS SQUAD DOES FOR FUN

Having scoured all of Ulan Bator for chocolate, it was gratifying to discover an almost inexhaustible supply of chocolate-wrapped almonds on the fourth floor of our hotel under the flexible custody of the Chief of the Mongolian Natural Disasters Rescue Squad. Flexible in the sense that you could buy a $2 bag of peanuts if you downed quart of vodka. At least it felt like a quart. The Chief flagged us down in the hotel laundry area. We must have borne the scars of our ongoing chocolate deprivation. There was an utterly tasteless irony about us craving chocolate in a land where everyone else craved the most basic staple foods. We knew this, but it just pushed our cravings underground. The Chief got us when we were most vulnerable with our greying underwear laid out on the heating pipes to dry. We would have gone anywhere with him to get him away from our laundry. He had a badge and a gold stripe on his shoulder so we knew we could trust him.

Upstairs three of his friends had worked their way through a pint of vodka each and were playing the kind of games with chocolate-coated almonds that children should never see. There was a strong tang of Old Spice in the air but we could still smell chocolate. Over vodka and almonds The Chief told us that usually Mongolian people are warm and welcoming and smily, but because of the economic depression right now they all looked sad and hostile. This was the first year that foreigners from the West had been allowed in to Mongolia, except rich executives from big oil companies who wanted to exploit the land and deprive Mongolia's nomadic farming population of its traditional hunting grounds. Plus, he told us, all Mongolian people were genuinely welcoming to foreigners and wanted to get to know us, not get at our money. We both stifled a pang of remorse for the friendly lady in the minty-fresh apartment who only wanted to send her daughter to China. Perhaps what we had at first seen as a national hostility or at best general wariness towards foreigners was explained by worry about their future (real worries, bread rations were down to two loafs a week and rice and flour had just started to be rationed) and an overwhelming sense of sadness at the deterioration of what The Chief described as their Once Great Country. The Mongolian Tugrik, explained the Chief, was practically worthless now. How could people ever get out now? Without an armed force or even a solid manufacturing base, he argued, Mongolia was vulnerable too to the predatory ambitions of China who already led armed poaching raids into the Mongolia outback to hunt snow leopards and reindeer. Mongolian people were proud he said, and didn't like to beg for money.

When a phone call from a friend who'd managed to lock himself in the bathroom called The Chief away (evidently the term "natural disaster" is fairly expansive) we wandered off to find a Mongolian bar. Lacking the inability to learn from previous mistakes but sure of safety in numbers (there were six of us) and confident that our new respect for Mongolian national pride would build us a million bridges we ran a gauntlet of drunken old men (largely slumbering under trees) in search of refreshment. There was only one bar in town, in a fairly characterless hotel for roaming Russian businessmen. It sold luxury western goods such as Lux soap and Colgate toothpaste in its lobby as well as stamps which we needed, so we stopped to peruse the selection. To our surprise the lady with the minty-fresh apartment was standing at the counter buying three pairs of nylons and some Jack Daniels whisky with a fat wad of American dollars. So much for our remorse!!

WHAT'S THE SIGN FOR "THERE'S A DOG UNDER YOUR BED?"

The next morning we endured a crazy bus ride through the potholes of the Mongolian countryside to reach a camp on the edge of Gobi Desert where we would pass the next week. When we finally arrived we all erupted in smiles just for the joy of being back in the countryside. Set in a valley between the most beautiful mountains, soft and rolling and painted in the colours of England in May with a shading of conifers along the mountain's spines and a forest of deciduous trees all lime greens and mustards along the river at the far back of the camp. At the back of the camp was a family of yurts and an animal pen huddled in a meadow painted all over with yellow and purple flowers. When we arrived they were skinning a sheep in a pen beside the water tap. Later there were two buckets of frothy pink innards sitting in the sun beneath the bloody pinned-out sheep-skin. Four or five little children, all dressed in traditional Mongolian clothes with base-ball caps shielding their eyes from the unrelenting sun, seemed to live around the yurts, waving and calling "hello" and "goodbye" as we clambered past.

Intoxicated with the clarity of the colours we were breathing we set off away from the yurts towards what we wildly hoped was the great outdoors. The sun on the edge of the desert was merciless, thirty degrees at least, and our shoulders blistered into bubble-wrap as we followed the winding road under a sky the colour of a peacock's tail with tiny scraps of fraying amber cloud skating along the shimmering horizon. A light wind fretted the bobbing blossoms that cavorted in the fields, dizzyingly yellow under the perfect sky. Adventurous, we set off the road and climbed a deceptively steep hill all bristling with grasses and reeds and fluttering purple petals whipped up by the wind.

At the top of the hill we found a lady for ever after referred to as The Mad Bonnet Lady. Of indiscernible nationality, with interrogating eyes, a mouth that could outperform an air-raid siren and a nose that knows no bounds, they had let her into the country one day and couldn't get her out. Once we heard her "halloo" s trumpeting over the hill, sending wildlife and small children scattering, our beautiful afternoon stroll became a thing of the past. Tenacious like a bug with suction-cup feet and indiscreet as an elephant in an aviary, she joined us for our walk. Unfortunately it was a long walk. After an hour or so we came down into a village where a party of friendly but slavering dogs attached themselves to us. They proved curiously pleasant company after the Mad Bonnet Lady's incessant horn-blowing. What awkwardness Laura and I felt blundering into the village, the Mad Bonnet Lady more than made-up for in gutsy, patronising arrogance. While she ruffled the hair of nursing mothers more than twice our age and tweaked their "quaint little frocks" , it was gratifying to see small children tried to lodge pebbles in her bonnet from their vantage point on top of a milk churn. Just as she tried, with lots of hearty hail and gusto, to show a strapping young Mongolian Horseman how to carry a saddle, a dog came bounding over the hill and sank its teeth into her ankle. It was not a deep bite, but it got her moving again.

Soon we came to the brow of a hill where beneath us opened a magical meadow valley peppered with sixty of so yurts each with a fragile plume of smoke spiralling up from its roof. The settlement nestled in the elbow where the plains met the mountains. We turned along the top of the hill and made our way back across the hill and down to the river where an elderly lady and a young girl of four or five were collecting something from the river, a burning sapphire blue under the afternoon sun. By this time we noticed that four of the original six dogs were still with us. They stayed with us all the way back to the camp and the Mad Bonnet Lady, for once, stayed quiet.

We had failed to take into account the bitter depths to which temperatures could plummet on the edge of the desert and as we rounded the hill that loomed over our camp, we all started rubbing our arms and legs. A biting wind seemed to have whipped itself up from nowhere and our sunburnt shoulders screamed as it sliced across our skin. We ran the last bit back to the yurt, anticipating that some kind of heating system and possibly a warm beverage would be waiting for us.

We were sharing a yurt with a friendly couple from Germany called Dana and Mark. The almost circular yurt was divided inside with four beds around the circumference and a stove in the middle with a large chimney taking the smoke up and outside. In our enthusiasm to explore we'd forgotten that we'd need to actually start the fire at some point if we wanted to get warm. "*You're in the country now, Sportsfans*" Russ would later warm us.

I leapt into bed as soon as we got back into the yurt to warm up, while Laura scurried around collecting fire-wood. It appears I actually fell asleep because when I next awoke the yurt was black as coal and all around me the ripples of gentle breathing from Dana and Mark and Laura and ......there was another sound in there, husky almost, rasping, with a curious bubbling undertone like a cappuccino-maker making froth. It seemed to be coming from under my bed. I crept onto my tiptoes and mustering all I could remember from *Carry On Screaming*, stole a very hesitant peek under my bed. Two big orange eyes burned back and I felt a warm, yet strangely foul-smelling rush of air on my cheek. My heart pounded and I all but stifled a scream. Trying to keep a calm handle on myself, I tried to rationalise that it could be a weasel or some other friendly woodland creature. I looked under the bed again. This time I heard a definite growl, a husky growl, that sounded like no squirrel I had ever met. I squealed and something dashed out from under the bed, brushing past me in a flurry of fur and something strange and sticky that flicked onto my leg. I tipped right over because my foot had gone to sleep and banged my head on the stove. This startled the beast, sending him spinning helter-skelter round the yurt, eventually coming to an asthmatic halt under Laura's bed.

I then realised that of course, this must be one of the dogs that had been following us since yesterday. I nudged open the yurt door to let some light in, letting out a convulsive shiver as an evil wind slashed through my T-shirt, and sent a hesitant scout foot out towards Laura's bed. I whispered softly to let her know I was coming. Finally I reached the edge of the bed after just one painful altercation with the stove, and dropped to my knees, landing nicely in a pool of dog froth. Just then, I sneezed, it came out of nowhere, shattering the eerie silence. Laura, at least I thought it was Laura, woke up and turned into Mark. Here I was in my night-shirt kneeling in a pool of dog dribble next to Dana's German husband. He sat bolt upright in bed quite freaked out as if I had been watching him sleep or something.

Fortunately the language barrier was not a problem as Dana and Mark were both deaf. I pantomimed my way in the darkness through the events of our day including the walk and the bit where we picked up the salivating dogs. That bit seemed to scare him. By this time everyone was awake and things are no clearer. Explaining to a deaf German lady in a pitch black yurt that a salivating dog was hiding out in the tent and that was why I was kneeling by her husband's bed was not at all easy. Eventually Mark, looking very cross and ruffled produced a flashlight and a small notepad. I shone the flashlight under the bed but the cunning hound had beat a hasty retreat when things started getting nasty. Mark threw his hands into the air. At least I think he did. It was very dark in there. Not knowing a single line in German except "my father is a tortoise" I drew a picture of a dog sneaking into our tent. Laura heard Mark whisper the German word for Cow under his breath but we weren't sure whether he thought I'd drawn a cow or thought I was a cow. Frozen now, and soaked in dog spit, I just went back to bed. Needless to say, no one slept easy for the next four nights. Our only gratification the following morning came from hearing that a large horse had bullied its way into the Mad Bonnet Lady's yurt in the middle of the night and taken a good chunk out of her bonnet.

IS THAT A SPIDER ON YOUR THIGH?

The next morning Laura and I decided to take ourselves off for a good sturdy walk, this time without the Mad Bonnet Lady and her endless rhetorical conversation. We set off along a different trail today, through a meadow ablaze with magnificent purple blooms and the usual yellow-green Mongolian grasses that reminded me of the colour of sugar cane in the fields of India. In the distance Mongolian horsemen in flashing red and orange robes dashed across the endless green on their curiously short-legged horses. We were never quite sure if they were hunting or just out for the ride.

We veered off to the right and headed up a short, but deceptively steep hill tangled with wiry grasses clung tenaciously to our shorts and T-shirts and stripped the hairs from our legs like no waxing treatment I had ever tried. Laura decided to scramble up the gentler but grassier slopes while I set off across the rocks where I suspected there would be less barbs to slash me. Just one last heave away from the top, I sensed something pulling my leg back down the hill. I couldn't take a step forward. I tried again, lunging forward athletically at the hip but my leg just wouldn't move. It was if I were suddenly tied down. Half-laughingly wondering if these curiously tenacious weeds were in fact an alien vegetable product and I'd be bound into a fat cocoon before I could shout "Mulder and Scully", I glanced down to see something like a tennis-net wound right around my thigh. I shuddered and made an impotent swipe to brush it from my legs. It was surprisingly sticky and as strong as duct tape. Suddenly, the appalling realisation struck that I was trapped in a spider's web. Now the trifidic grasses with their cocoon-building skills seemed delightfully innocuous. From the size and strength of the web I extrapolated that the spider must be at least ten inches in diameter. Just at that moment, out of the corner of my eye, I noticed something black, and round and shiny, with eight little wizened legs that would seem to have no long term survival value, sitting on my leg. A spider with a brilliant red cross etched on its beetle-black body sat right on the edge of my shorts. There was about one millimetre between its waving little front leg and the bare skin of my upper thigh. Some demented reflex drew my hand to my leg and I swiped the magnificent creature back into the bushes feeling just a little click as I touched it. Then I let out a maniacal wolf-like howl that brought Laura scrambling to the peak to look down at me. I leapt, like a cat on a hot tin-roof, across boulders and bristling grasses, near hysterical and scrabbling all the time at my legs like a madman on LSD imagining beetles swarming all over him. When I finally caught up with Laura I was trembling like the pathetic phobic that I was. Every grass that brushed against me had me swatting maniacally at my arms, legs, ankles and sweating from places I didn't know could sweat. It took us quite a time to get to the very top of the hill, with me skipping and hopping every inch of the way like a demented chorus-line girl.

DECOMPOSING DAIRY PRODUCTS: MY FAVOURITE!

By our third day in the yurt everything smelt of mutton and I was glad to get onto an animal that wasn't a goat. In fact it was a horse, a tempestuous beauty with an iron neck, an asbestos mouth and a will of steel, who would take me to a village just two miles away to collect milk for the camp. The term "saddle" in Mongolian may well be synonymous with "razor blade" given the ridge of highly polished leather we were given to "rest" ourselves on. The overall effect was rather like trying to sit on a cheesewire. Anatomical profiling was a concept evidently yet to reach the Mongolian Steppes. Or perhaps people were built differently in this part of the world with their genitalia set in huge vaulted recesses approximately six inches deep.

We retraced our path from yesterday across the brow of the hill and into the village beyond. Overall, I felt much safer on a horse, although the really long grasses still made me twitch a little. In the village a lady who claimed to be the mother of one of the Mongolians in our camp welcomed us into her house with lots of friendly backslapping and handshaking. We were invited to sit on tiny six-inch stools in front of a massive steel-framed hospital style bed. On the walls around the bed stethoscopes and blood pressure gauges hung from spindly screws. I wondered if she were some kind of Doctor. Surprisingly one wall was covered with dated colour photographs and glossy pictures carved out of magazines showing what appeared to be

Ulan Bator at its entrepreneurial heights, lots of men in suits and magnificent ministerial banquets, a party in the town square and some kind of dinosaur being wheeled through the main streets wrapped in a big red ribbon. It brought home to us how much things had changed for Mongolia over the last few years.

It was a tremendous honour for us to be invited into their home, and we tried to express our appreciation in lots of grovelly ways that probably got lost in the translation. "Tea" offered Mrs Khan proffering an inoffensive looking teapot and a teaspoon. "Mmmmm, yes please" we gushed like something out of the famous five. She mimed that she would bring snacks too for our refreshment. Mmmmm, we chorused again, with a trace of hesitancy this time. The tea came, with a nice thick film of grease on top. Mm- And a couple of hairs. Oh, yes, and a fly for added nutrient. Trying to look culturally aware I questioned our host at length about the contents of Mongolian chai. Apparently, we think she told us, they use butter instead of milk. Mare's milk butter ,that is. Ohhh, goodie, snack time. Mrs Khan came out of the cooking area laden down with a veritable stash of decomposing mare's milk products, including a very sticky cheese and Mongolia's national alcoholic beverage - fermented mare's milk, which tasted surprisingly innocuous, like a rather runny yoghurt. It certainly explained the difference in dental quality between the Mongolians, avid dairy fiends of the Central Asian Steppe, and the Japanese people we'd known with their endless deteriorating enamel stories.

On the way home, pumped full of decaying horse product and uncomfortably bilious, two small children soothed our minds if not our buttocks with a gentle ballad that causes much merriment among the Mongol speaking adults. We were sure we could hear our names among the river of Mongolian words flowing over the valley.

HAVE YOU TRIED MONGOLIAN VODKA?

That night, in the true spirit of the Mongolian outback, the men on our camp slaughtered a goat. They made a neat slit in its abdomen which they put their hand through to cut clean through one of its main arteries, apparently a very clean and efficient way of killing it. We couldn't, or wouldn't watch the actual slaughter. While the head bubbled pleasantly on the open fire, they stripped the meat from the carcass and placed it in a kind of cast-iron pressure cooker with layers of hot coals, then meat, then chilli powder, then hot coals, then meat, then chilli powder, then hot coals, then meat.....until the pot was full. Then the lid was tightly buttoned down and we settled down to wait for dinner. In the meantime the skin was carefully stripped clean and hung up to dry while a four or five year old girl supping from a can of Tiger Beer used the head in a succession of disappointing practical jokes. Apparently infantile alcoholism was a big problem in Mongolia. It was easy to see why.

After twenty minutes or so, when the girl became dizzy and got bored of the goat's head, the iron pot was hauled by four or five men over to another yurt where we hesitantly feasted on goat's blood broth and chunks of dark, red goat meat from the bone, all washed down with a swig of Chinese vodka. Our Mongolian host sternly chastised his four year old daughter for trying to mix her drinks. The vodka burnt away the taste of the goat as well as most of the cells lining our throat cavity. Given the Mongolians' rejection of all thing considered Chinese (for example bicycles and certain kinds of mushroom) it was surprising that Chinese vodka was so accepted. I asked our Mongolian host about this. His reply - "have you tried Mongolian vodka??" said it all. I remembered how The Chief had described Genghis Khan Vodka as best absorbed slowly through the skin. On no accounts, he warned us, with all the authority of a man who knows about Natural Disasters, should you drink the stuff!!!

Just at that moment, a yak came blundering into the yurt. Our host explained that they were usually vegetarians and that we shouldn't be worried. Being in the company of an angry yak with a blood lust did nothing to increase my enjoyment of the evening's sordid proceedings, amazing as it was to have been part of a ritual feast that was as old, they said, as the Gobi desert. The yak looked like a living My Little Pony with a big swishy tail that little girls would die to plait and an unfeasibly small and bog-eyed head. It looked like a hybrid between a lama and a Persian kitten. Laura had bought an assortment of rancid yak-hair products during our travels in Mongolia and was quite excited to finally see one.

However, our speculative cogitations on the evolutionary origins of the yak were interrupted by the goat-slayer (surprisingly a man called Khan) suddenly leaping into the air, screaming loudly and trying to batter Shaun the super-nice Lancastrian with his fire-poker. It transpired, after some general mayhem and a small amount of bloodshed

(Shaun was prone to nose-bleeds when upset), that Shaun had gotten Mr Khan to look into his video camera, wherein he saw himself, in miniature, bringing a goat back to life. First he put its head back on, then he ran backwards round a field while the goat cavorted with its friends in the meadow. Shaun, trying to explain simultaneously the concepts of electromagnetic media and rewind-play, came desperately unstuck with his inadequate selection of four Mongolian words, two of which featured toilets. Convinced that some kind of satanic power was contained in this white-man's devil box (we think that's what he was saying) Mr Khan bolted from the tent screaming loudly. He came back with a wary grimace several minutes later and a large stick. Shaun looked nervous and stuffed an extra Kleenex up his nose as a precautionary measure. He had the video camera ready to play in forward mode this time, at regular speed. It took lots of gentle coaxing to bring Mr Khan back to the table but once he got the idea there absolutely no stopping him. Malcolmn Khan Spielberg was born that night under the stars on the Mongolian plain. We were all menaced by his probing lens as we "enjoyed" various savoury goat parts and tried desperately hard to avoid sitting next to the Mad Bonnet Lady who said soothing things like "There, you see. Civilisation's not so bad" to a large man with an empty bottle of Genghis Khan and what seemed to be some kind of scimitar. Bed could not come soon enough.

SIBERIA

The sky that night was full of stars and Orion looked close enough to grope. The plains rolled endlessly into the night, the flicker of lights from our fourteen carriages dancing across the tussocks and stone. The popular pretty girls in the compartment next door were having a party, and the flashes of cameras and pearly-white teeth were thankfully swallowed up by the darkness outside. We had been invited, but with a sneer. It was like school all over again. Still, I was feeling very romantic like some adventuring 19th century Helena-Bonham-Carter in warm stockings and boned knickers. I would, of course, be called Kate or Margaret, something solid and reassuring yet winsomely feminine. I'd have some kind of bonnet contraption perched on my head and a fairly hefty set of corsets, the way those early women travellers did. And perhaps an attractive set of matching leather luggage embossed with my initials in pure gold leaf and a man-servant called

Harley to bring me hot milk while I scribbled in a leather-bound journal about the howling wolves and devilish winds.

Instead I was nursed up with a cup-a-soup in an old pair of jogging bottoms listening to the thumps and throbs of a party that had achieved a record of eighteen people crammed into one four-berth compartment. Russ had burst in earlier looking wild-eyed looking for coffee to cloud the sting of his Genghis Khan vodka. Anna Marie, who'd just spent four months travelling around Asia, was drinking anything she could find to console herself following the disappearance of a large yellow bag stuffed with all her diving gear from the train at the previous stop. The ladies who serviced our compartment evidently knew something about something, but we were fresh out of pottery horses and Marlborough cigarettes. Information could not be bought with smiles alone. Strangely, it was the most conspicuous bag I had ever seen, resembling a large neoprene banana approximately six feet long, and it was unlikely that anyone could have picked it up by mistake. We had been warned that people sometimes sneaked on board at the scheduled stops and rifled through the compartments while the occupants stretched their legs but we were all amazed that we hadn't seen anyone walking away under her bag. Unless, hinted Russ with one of his rare flashes of cunning and insight, the man who stole Claire's bag had an even bigger bag in which to conceal her yellow bag. This would make the thief's bag the size of a small articulated lorry. We were fairly sure we'd have seen that too.

So, while The Love Shack hammered through the compartment walls and the stars grew brighter outside, I sat up and ruminated in a delicious moment of private introspection that was rare on a trip like this. The moment seemed unblemishable, because neither I, watching the stars reel by, or the world outside, too big to be bothered by me, could harm one another in either way. There was a refreshing lack of cause and effect here, just the endless, and insignificant cogitations of a spectator watching one of the largest, unblemished expanses of natural wilderness spin inexorably by.

THREE WAYS TO LOSE YOUR PASSPORTS!

My tranquil reflections of the previous evening was smeared into oblivion at about three o'clock the next morning when another interminable probe by steely-eyed customs and immigration inspectors shattered my dreams. This time three potato-coloured visa-inspectors in vicious blue eye-shadow (one of whom resembled my little-spoken-about Uncle Colin) stabbed us with their clipboards while we shook off the bleariness of sleep. They all had eerily pale blue eyes and not for the first time I issued a telepathic plea to Agent Mulder. Feeling a hollow bravado in numbers, despite the fact that as pasty-faced foreigners in a range of fleecy nightwear we were in fact in the vulnerable position, we asked them each in turn about Anna-Marie's yellow bag. Each one of them glittered his or her sparkly blue eyes in the darkness and gave us a truly Russian scowl. Russ, his senses happily drink-smudged - sat up in his bunk and began a rousing chorus of Edelweiss for which there was little collective approval. The visa-officer let out a small scream as he leapt to the floor to menace her with his rolling red-eyes and unRussian underwear. While she tried to bat at him with her clipboard, her friend blew a whistle which woke the whole train. We tried in vain to persuade Russ that this lady was just trying to look friendly, (in that tight-lipped way peculiar to government officials who are up all through the night), and did not in fact want to join his one-man Conga line. In that one night Russ did more, or less for Russian-US relations than any US Ambassador had ever done in a lifetime.

By the time we extricated ourselves from the piercing scrutiny of the inspectors (they looked a bit like a sixties backing group with their dyed hair and blue eye-shadow) it was nearly morning . The train was now speeding through Siberia. In our mental library we had a sterile semi-Arctic landscape patrolled by the occasional tiger and perhaps a little Eskimo neatly logged against "Siberia". But to our surprise, the soil was a little sandy, evidently a Russian influence given the coloration of the passport inspectors, and the landscape was scoured by brooding pine-covered mountains and endless grassy swamps, painstakingly cultivated on the higher ground by men with scythes and muscley calves and sturdy wagons. From the window we could make out intermittent flashes of yellow, oil seed rape perhaps, or sunflowers, glinting along the horizon. It was all very unarctic.

Hungry now after our early start, we waited and waited and waited for the dining car to open. A man called Jean-Pierre with a little goatee beard who must surely have been The Count of Bismarck in a previous life, produced some dry bread and cherry jam and shared it round the carriages. This was good as we were unable to face any more noodles, and Russ's seven boxes of dried fruit had started to lose their appeal. Both Malcolm and Russ had been suffering from a particularly intractable case of constipation which they attribute solely to the excessive desiccation of the dried banana slices. Malcolm claimed to have experienced no tangible or gaseous output for three days. "I feel as tight as a helium balloon" he moaned. Laura and I had decided to save our jam and chocolate nuts in case the carriage attendants started getting nasty and upped their demands. Already we had given them all the photos from our guide book, a drawing of my cat and an empty cassette case. Grimly we wondered how nasty things could get by the time we arrived in Moscow. We'd both seen Lord of the Flies and that grim Danish film where desperate sailors drink each other's urine. We didn't think we were ready to make the ultimate sacrifice.

Plus or minus six hours, we spent most of the day not knowing what time it was, and waiting for lunch or breakfast or dinner to be served. At around 2.00 p.m. Mongolian time, the last reliable time zone we were in, breakfast was finally announced (once the "trading" sign had been removed from the door and a man with a goat, three loaves of bread and some suspicious newspaper-wrapped packages finally left the dining car). The choices that morning were raw beetroot, Borsch (thinly disguised beetroot), beetroot sandwiches (without the bread) and beetroot flan (without the pastry case). We made a point of being extra nice to the Count of Bismarck for the rest of the day.

Eventually we drew to a stop in an tiny industrial town called Zagustay flanked by ugly black factories that belched smoke into the air. We leapt off, the first chance in ages to stretch our legs, and found a lady selling herbed boiled potatoes wrapped in newspaper and tiny bundles of fresh sweet raspberries in little cardboard punnets. We wandered along the platform enjoying the warmth of the sun on our backs and the taste of the world's most delectable raspberries. Never, ever, had food tasted so good. Being British, we were used to the superior taste of potato products eaten directly from newspaper but these boiled potatoes surprised even us with their salty richness. While we sauntered along, in a pleasant state of calorie-induced reverie, we didn't notice all the other people slowly climbing back onto the train. Not until we heard that mighty groan. To our absolute horror we watched the sand-dusted wheels of the mighty locomotive lurch into movement. We screamed, and belted back towards the carriages where we hammered on the doors and screamed into the deafening roar of the engine. But the wheels kept moving. Inside were our passports, our money, our flight tickets, our luggage, and everything important that we owned. Just as we all but broke down, the train's whistle screeched and with a hell-like scream of brakes and a rush of steam the eerie grating on steel on steel drowned out our hysterical pleas. The train stopped. Embarrassed now by our own hysteria, we climbed red-faced and coolly nonchalant (yeah, we knew it was going to stop...) back onto the train.

Two hours later, at about five o'clock we stopped at a town called Slyndyanka, which sits about half a mile from the rim of Lake Baikal, the largest fresh water lake in the world, a mile deep in places and populated by a unique species of fresh-water seal found nowhere else in the world. We'd been skirting the periphery of the lake all afternoon. Slydyanka station itself was conspicuously unattractive squatting at it did in the centre of an old mining town. The general air of dereliction that swamped the town seemed to have unhinged its residents, who largely wore synthetic leopard skin furs and footless tights and straining stiletto heels. All the women seemed to have had their hair permed and bleached at some earlier date and wore the ubiquitous vivid blue eye-makeup which made Slyndyanka a prime target for extra-terrestrial colonisation.

Within seconds of the wheels stopping a hundred small children swarmed into our compartment asking for pens and cigarettes and chewing gum. Chewing gum seems to be high on the list of tradable commodities on this leg of the trip, after nylons in a range of fetching American tan hues. (Evidently there is a higher aesthetic standard here than in the streets of Beijing. Laura offered a Russian lady a small packet of popsocs and she all but spat contemptuously in her face.) There was a tremendous clatter of noise all around us, people shouting and hawking and heckling. Looking down the length of the train we saw that all the Mongolians, careful not to leave their carriages, hung Western-brand trainers, A-line nylon skirts, sports tops, anoraks, huge padded Parkas and T-shirts out of the windows. A great cloud of local people had gathered under each window shouting prices and waving notes and carrying their wares back to show their friends and families. Around the edge of the platform station guards stood around, taking no notice of anything that was going on. Laura and I packed up our passports and remaining hard currency and got ready to go onto the platform to stretch our legs.

Just at that moment a crew of three body-building Russians with bulging necks stormed into our compartment with empty shopping bags demanding to know what we were selling. They were quite intimidating with their hairy arms and curious habit of spitting to the side before speaking (thankfully onto Russ's mattress). "Sell passport?". "Passport sell?". "Sell sell passport passport?". They seemed to be working their way through every permutation of sell and passport. "No sell, no sell" we said quietly, all the while looking for a secret door-release mechanism that might drop us down onto the tracks where we could hide until the Russians went away. "Sell T-shirt?" growled one of the them with a sinister leer over his shoulder and a less than spectacular ejection of flem which lodged in his beard and quivered menacingly while he snorted and rifled through Malcolm's sheets. "No sell" we said again, moving hesitantly towards the men. We secretly hoped to chase them away with our less than sweet smell but they were made of stronger stuff. "This sell?" gruffed one of the other men. Amazingly, he wanted to buy Malcolm's stinky toilet bag. "No sell" said Laura, with the utmost propriety. "How much?" said I, with a mind for a quick bargain coupled with the added bonus of the indefinite removal of Malcolm's facecloth. They passed it between them with lots of speculative huhs and gruff manly hawking sounds. They each solemnly sniffed the facecloth, and seemed to find it pleasing. One man took Malcolm's deodorant stick and dabbed it hesitantly on his wrists. I thought it was a guaranteed sale but just at that moment Malcolm came bursting back into the compartment to find the contents of his washbag under the close scrutiny of three very big men in leather braces. Laura and I tried to look whimpering and innocent and made a point of cowering slightly. Just then, the Prodyostna (carriage attendant) let out a surprisingly loud bellow that reverberated through the train and the corridors suddenly filled with lots of burly Russian men clambering to get into her boudoir. The three Russians in our compartment gave us a fairly unimpressed scowl before joining the throng in the corridor. We are sure to this day that we saw a small man in a raincoat walking off with a small pottery horse and a young child clutching a picture of Peter Ustinov astride a small gazelle.

A BRUSH WITH BANDITS?

It was about three o'clock in the morning when the earth-shattering screech of metal grating on metal shook us from our slumbers and sent Laura and I tumbling from our bunks on to the floor. The train screamed as it slammed to a snails pace, and with a last few reticent grunts and groans jerked and jolted to a stop. The metallic echo of the wheels clanking and a door at the front of the train slamming rattled through the eerie stillness of our compartment. We all lay there in silence, brushing the last traces of dreams from our sleep-blurred minds. I had been enjoying a very unCatholic experience with a Mongolian goatherd but the moment was lost. "What the **** was that?" bellowed Russ with all the military authority of a large Texan roused suddenly from sleep. The train continued to rock slightly from side to side, its wheels complaining grumpily as they expanded and contracted with a series of loud bangs that seemed to be coming right through our walls. There were no other sounds of life.

Then people starting to murmur in the compartment next to us, we could hear their urgent whispers through the wall. Just then someone knocked on our door with what sounded like an elaborately coded system of raps. Either that or this was some kind of musical trivial pursuits - what famous 1950's show tune followed this amusing little Rumba rhythm? ...."Who is it?" bellowed Russ. Again - knock—kno-kno-kno-knock- knock ————knock knock. Russ leapt from bed and flung open the door. "What the ****?" he bellowed into the petrified blackness. "Shhhh Shhhhhhh" whispered a scared little voice from somewhere down by the floor. It was Shaun, the innocuous man from Lancaster. "Don't turn your lights on. Don't say a word. I will repeat this only once. We think it might be bandits". "Hmmmmm" grunted Russ, scratching his head and feeling altogether less bold. "Jean-Pierre's Dad did this exact route a couple of months ago", continued Russ, "and his train was stopped three times. We must hunker down and button down our hatches. Spread the word". With that he was gone, off to wake Claire and Miranda.

So we lay in absolute darkness our imaginations fomenting all kinds of punishments involving yaks and elastic bands, the only items of torture other than scimitars we had seen in the last month. I wondered about swallowing my jewellery but knew this was no place to stage a toilet sit-in. (Conditions had deteriorated to the point of desperation. People had been seen urinating from train windows despite the uncomfortable backwind and the risk of splashing a burly Mongolian enjoying the fresh Siberian air three carriages down). Somewhere at the front of the train we heard shouting. Or was it murderous screaming. We pictured our friendly little train driver (we'd never seen him but now he seemed like family) held with a scimitar blade to his throat while laughing, swaggering bandits made him eat a succession of indigestible potato products. They could take my pleasantly fleecy pyjamas, my silk suit from Hong Kong, my stash of magic Chinese tea, but not my passport. I hid it under my mattress just to be sure. Just then Malcolm woke up with a high-pitched squeal later attributed to a small pocket of trapped wind and we all jumped two feet into the air. For Laura and Russ this meant hitting their heads on the ceiling. From outside (was Shaun outside our door again?) we heard an urgent Shhhhhh.

Just then we heard someone crunch along the gravel outside our carriage, slow steady footsteps that didn't sound like they'd take "will you take this small iron waste-paper basket instead?" for an answer. Then voices again, right outside our window. We lay there for I don't know how long just waiting for the tap of a gun on our window. I gave myself a serious talking to about the sacrifices one can be called upon at any time to make for the sake of one's friends and achieved a measure of peace with myself just as the footsteps started crunching away. Two minutes later we heard the whirr of the engine kick into gear . We never did find out why the train stopped or who the men with the crunchy feet were, but evidently it made a deep impact of Malcolm's subconscious. Later that night he was heard to mumble "Don't touch Lassie, take me instead" from the murkiest recesses of his dreams.

ALL AGLOW WITH REVOLUTIONARY ZEAL

That afternoon we staged a coup. We think it was unheard of in all the history of the Trans-Siberian-Railroad but there was no-one around to corroborate our suspicions (except a very old man who waited in the dining car and he refused to enter into any conspiracy that might invoke the anger of the carriage goddesses. Apparently one of them had some kind of medical background and could do nasty things with a sharpened breadfruit).

It started when Laura locked herself in the toilet. The carriage attendant, upon receipt of a box of dried fruit pieces, gave me a door handle which attached to the door and released the locking mechanism inside. Her mistake was to turn her back on me. It was the moment I'd been waiting for and with a schoolgirl's glee at my own daring impertinence I secreted the large and uncomfortably cold piece of metal up my sweater. After liberating my friend from the less than sanitary washroom we sidled quickly back to our compartment while the carriage attendant searched frantically for the handle. Without the handle, their key was as impotent as a fish's wet bits on a wet day. We moved swiftly, hiding the handle carefully in Shaun, the innocuous Lancastrian's, compartment. Having spent two days pantomiming our lavatorial urgencies to the carriage attendant (she liked to see nothing less than real pain; tears could really boost a flagging appeal), we felt no remorse about seizing guardianship of the toilet. Indeed we were quite aglow with revolutionary zeal for the next few hours. There was a certain self-righteous satisfaction in wrestling control of our most intimate bodily functions from a short, round lady in black who had almost made us cry.

Unfortunately, as with any great revolution, a certain amount of anarchy ensued while the reins of power changed hands. People drifted rudderless and cross-legged for a couple of hours before the official announcement was made from the upper bunk. Shaun basked in his new found popularity as puppet custodian of the door handle for few hours. Then things started to deteriorate. People were abusing their new found freedom. One man from Strasbourg went four times in one hour and left a nasty blockage situation for the next occupant. Reports of three or even four people in the washroom at any one time were not actually authenticated but we do know that the Count of Bismarck paid handsomely in pop-tarts for an unquestioned thirty minute claim to the toilet that very afternoon. His latest love, a flimsy woman called Caroline, was reported to be missing too.

Our initial hopes that democracy would prevail in the battle for guardianship of the door handle proved fundamentally flawed. There were people on that train who were hungry for power. Apparently the plotting started within hours of the coup, but, as is always the way, we were too blind to see. We'd chosen Shaun as puppet-head custodian because he seemed neutral in so many ways, but already they were people ready to use him as a helpless pawn in their ruthless games, levying an unofficial chocolate-almond tax on this most basic of bodily functions. By nightfall things had reached a crisis situation. We were forced to issue a sharp crackdown on the conspirators (we knew who they were) by seizing control of the key ourselves and hiding it in an empty packet of dried fruit bits under Malcolm's mattress. We knew that no-one would go there unless they were really really desperate. But then someone, (again, we knew who) took a screwdriver to the toilet door which made our door handle obsolete and left the power in the hands of a dangerous man with aristocratic pretensions, a goatee beard and a screwdriver. People are fickle as flies in a dungfield. Within minutes of the rumour, they were fluttering around the big goatee-bearded pile of XXXX proffering peppermints and noodles that seemed to come from nowhere. It was all getting very unegalitarian.

Eventually at around seven o'clock we had to convene an emergency meeting in the corridor. To this day I think we handled it rather well. We took the screwdriver, (of course there were protests at first.......) and affixed the door handle back on the door, which seemed to appeal to everybody's natural sense of order. We then took some curiously gelatinous putty that Shaun found in his rucksack (he thought it had been some kind of food product in an earlier life) and blocked the key hole. Now we, and the carriage attendants (who'd admittedly been looking a little cross-eyed for the last couple of hours), could defecate at will and the ugly heckling for power that had brought out the best and worst in all of us was never spoken of again.

TOGAS AND TUNDRA IN EXILE

Malcolm and Russ finally relieved their constipation problems today, Malcolm more spectacularly with a loud scream and a whole roll of toilet paper, which Russ was not at all gracious about given the scarcity of such rations on this train. Russ had dropped his walkman earlier and had spent the whole afternoon listening to the sounds of small chipmunks eating away at his REM tape. It appeared to have made him hyper but we were all careful not to notice. We stopped in Tomsk this afternoon, where Dostoyevsky had spent four years doing hard labour for political crimes back in 1849. (Malcolm had bought a book that dealt out carefully measured nuggets of information about the Trans-Siberian railway. You had to match the mile number posted at the side of the track with the relevant page in the book, which kept him busy for hours. We found his little pearls of wisdom quite amusing, largely given the paucity of alternative entertainment options in the wastelands of tundric Siberia, but Russ was running on a very small fuse today following a sordid and apparently disappointing upper-bunk encounter with Caroline the previous night. Apparently her "thing" with the Count of Bismarck was through. She was one of those foxy, sexually-confident women who could make the word "cup-a-soup" sound like something you'd scream during raw, animal sex. Naturally we didn't like her).

Dostoyevsky, Malcolm continued, received a generous flogging for complaining about the mud in his soup. Evidently Siberia's canteens in the late 19th century were little better-stocked than now. Being from Oklahoma, and therefore obligated to drawl, it took Malcolm a long time to finish complicated sentences. He managed to draw Dostoyevsky out for about seven seconds. Laura and I had taken to finishing words for him which he took very well but it still took several tedious hours to learn how the Russians used to exile their country-men to Siberia for such innocuous crimes as fortune-telling, taking snuff and driving a carriage with reins. The last one made perfect sense but the others seemed a little esoteric. If those old ministerial red-necks could see some of the things that had been going on in our compartment we'd all have been hanged. I could see the court proceedings now:

"It was today reported that a group of forty-seven people of varying Northern American and European extraction terrorised the people of Irkutsk by appearing on the station at 2 o'clock in the morning donned only in togas and some cherry-flavoured lipbalm. They proceeded to toast Lenin and sing Edelweiss in a loud and rousing chorus, baring all when the wind blew. Two local people, one selling a set of Russian dolls and the other a bottle of black-market Russian champagne, watched in bewilderment as a man resembling the Count of Bismarck played "Pass the Polo" with three of his flimsy young groupies. They were all sentenced to seventy three years of hard labour with the little Goatee One to be sold to into slavery in the Court of Khan the Horrible Avenger where he will wait on a small family of yaks and make cheese balls".

In actual fact the worst fate to greet the Count of Bismarck was a particularly tenacious Jack Russell terrier who took a misplaced fancy to his exposed knees, and an old Siberian woman who tried to sell him some nylons.

Wife-beating and drunkenness also became exilable offences in the early nineteenth century, more to fuel the increasing need for convicts to work in the mines than to address serious social issues. In the eighteenth century the exile system became a little more organised and forwarding prisons as well as proper exile stations were established at Tyumen and Tomsk. Some prisoners went from there to Irkutsk or to Sakhalin, the islands just north of Japan. The conditions sounded a little better than those in our compartment, with water at least (the water in the toilet cistern had finally dried up, fermenting much general animosity towards Malcolm after his early-morning purge.) The political exiles seemed to have the best deal, as they could set up home where they liked as long as it was in Siberia. Being used to England, a country roughly the size of an average 19th century Siberian farm, that seemed an infinite area in which to settle. We were particularly interested, (all things being relative) to learn how selected political exiles were sentenced to life-bondage into the Yakut Tribe of the Arctic Circle which must have been something of a shock after the frippery of the St Petersburg Court.

The whole exile system was temporarily abolished in the 1900s but under Stalin's regime, huge slave-labour camps were built in the 30s and 40s where the mortality rate was on average about thirty percent. Even today, there are apparently still some corrective labour camps in the Siberia but they are not, we hear, as severe as in days of old. It all seemed a world away from the vast, silver-birch splashed marshlands that had run alongside the train all day. Siberia for us meant adventure, largely experienced from the relative safety of our compartment, and a mounting sense of excitement to be nearing home. That and the unusual privilege of having no choice over the people you ate, drank and slept with for approximately two weeks. For people travelling the other way, a couple of hundred years ago, the journey must have meant something utterly, utterly different. The smells, one suspects, would probably have been much the same.

ANYONE SEEN A MAN WITH A MONKEY?

By the time our train slunk into the official Urals, (which always sounds strangely anatomical and tickled Malcolm into a paroxysm of schoolboy giggles), the scenery had become much more European, not in the sense of men in tights and foppish caps leaping alongside the train but deciduous trees and dog-roses and fields aflush with oil-seed rape with hawthorns in the hedgerows. It all suddenly felt very very familiar.

The houses were low here, hewn from precariously stacked piles of logs trussed together with a cunning mesh of rope and some kind of congealed potato product. Potatoes seemed to feature heavily in the dining car menu from the moment we entered the Urals (titter titter). Its peculiar adhesive qualities were soon confirmed by Russ who'd hidden a couple of spuds in his pocket in anticipation of a terminal decline in food quality as we neared Moscow. A small squeal was heard later that night when in the privacy of a small tent he'd crafted from his bedding roll he used a flashlight and a small pocket penknife to slice himself free. At least that's what he told us he was doing. Someone else was reported to have mended in a gaping hole in a neoprene wetsuit with just a slaver of the Head Chef's mash. At every tiny village stop people with rough skins burst forth from derelict railway carriages and rusting ladas to proffer sacks of spuds. The landscape, the people, and even the strangely pasty cows that simmered lightly in the fields under a blistering daytime sun, all seemed to take on the character of the unofficial national vegetable as our train sped through the Urals with a rush of metal and scream of steam (which was alarming as the train was allegedly electric) like an enormous zipper patching the Russian countryside into squares of yellow and brown and brilliant blue.

As we neared Moscow a treacherous and perhaps inevitable shift in the balance of power started to ensue. It started when almost casually one morning Russ opened up one of his strangely rhetorical and invariably senseless discourses on our plans on arrival at Moscow. We had given approximately three seconds worth of thought to this in the last two years as we'd never really expected to get as far as Moscow. It was touching, in a curious sort of way, this sudden surge of interest in our welfare but we were careful not to keep our hackles sharp and prickly. Justifiably so, we were gratified to note later, when our carefully gleamed intelligence corroborated our deepest suspicions. Someone, had something, that some other people were not allowed to have. It was the old gym locker story all over again. Caroline, the bewitchingly feline goddess-woman - (who'd taken such a liking to her toga that she'd worn it for many days since, to the incensement of all the weak-chinned, stubby fingered, soggy bellied men who jostled to ride opposite her in the dining car) - had very gently explained to Russ that she was actually dating a man who swallowed fire, tamed lions, and did something dubious with a monkey in a sparkly bikini on a high-wire in the name of Art. She made Art sound very grave indeed. She'd met him when the Russian Circus toured Europe (she was from one of those limp, sanitary mid-European countries like Luxembourg who long for lusty men and real body odour) and they had a shared this raw animal passion thing and now he was coming to meet her from the Train in Moscow.

Russ mustn't, she cautioned, in her Beatrice Potter voice, imagine he was in any kind of physical danger from the man who changed the face of the human cannonball act by dispensing with the cannon and throwing the ball himself. Anyway, she explained, like Goldilocks just before she killed all the bears and stole their furniture, Russ must consider their brief embarkation on the Ship of Incredible Passion a lusty sojourn on life's otherwise sexless, endlessly deteriorating highway. There was little in that sentence to console him, so he flung her some scathing rhetoric about not needing the help of any Russian strong-man and came back into our cabin to start kicking the door jam in the manner of say, Robert de Niro or Al Pacino, his cranium pink and shiny like a very small gobstopper as we looked up at him from my bunk. Perceptively we identified that he wasn't happy but we wasn't in the mood for sharing a confidence. So he paced up and down, up and down, up and down, in the small airgap between our compartment and the window on the other side of the corridor, for about three hours, which drove us all quite quite mad. By the end of that day we were all ready to eat fire and dance with small monkeys.

PLEASE PLEASE CAN WE JOIN THE CIRCUS??

The afternoon that we were due to arrive in Moscow, the train drew to a lurching, squealing halt outside a small village populated entirely by cows and a small man with a long stick, and didn't move again for six hours. Unfortunately, the Ministry for the Containment of Malodorous Foreigners would not permit us to get off and stretch our legs lest, presumably, we offend a small herd of benign-looking Jersey cattle and a whippety dog called Spittle. We railed and railed against this custodial heavy-handedness but none of us were man enough to just open the door and step right out. Each one of us feared that the train would move as soon as we got off. At least we could open the cabin window without the usual carcinogenic black smoke belching in and depositing a sooty microfilm on everything we owned. So all four of us clambered up to the window and enjoyed the rural sweetness of silage and dung in our nostrils.

When, eventually, we pulled into Moscow's Yaroslavl Railway Station, we were running over eight hours late. It was two o'clock in the morning. All our hopes that there would be small women with cosy bed-and-breakfasts vying for our custom were rudely dashed when instead we saw just five burly Russian men with bulging biceps and craggy Gillette-advert faces waiting next to a small Lada mini-van. They looked quite menacing. Caroline ran to them with a scream and wetted each of their faces with very unsisterly kisses. Russ stubbed his toe into a stopcock and stifled a grimace as his flip-flops heroically bore the brunt of his anger for the very last time (he would spend the next six days walking around Moscow haunted by the giggles of small children and the endless slap and flap of trailing rubber). We wondered if Caroline had acquainted herself with each of their Acts.

Russ squirmed as she flounced over all bouncy headed and springy-hipped like one of those unnatural women from the hairspray adverts to introduce Boris to her "friends". We tried to scowl for Russ's sake but knew there was a fundamental survival value in keeping Caroline sweet. While Russ turned away to study his guidebook (a pointless task given the darkness) we fawned and grovelled and looked vulnerable and needy. (We had perfected that by now). As she cheerfully loaded her luggage into the van we ingratiated ourselves as completely and pathetically as possible, vying over who should carry her dirty laundry bag, her stale coffee cup....We were spineless and utterly utterly cowardly.

Just then Jean-Pierre The Count of Bismarck sidled over. Did we have the address of The Intourist Hotel? We scathingly replied that we didn't know what he was talking about. Every foreigner staying in Moscow is legally obliged (obliged sounded benign enough, forced at gun-point would have sounded much more scary, though apparently the end-result is much the same) to stay in one the Intourist Hotels, Intourist being the Russian Tourist Agency. How much might that be, we bleated squeakily. One, maybe two hundred US a night...he speculated, No maybe 180.... or was it 160..... His pointless deliberations mattered little to us with our small bundle of one dollar notes and a Mastercard that had politely declined to stretch our funding capabilities. We might wangle an hour's sleep if they offered by the minute billing There was no way we could afford to stay in one of their fancy hotels. So what were we going to do for the next four nights?

Just then a large Russian man with a very small Coca-Cola shouted "I can take five". He was one of the fire-eating party. Laura and I tried to surge to the front. Caroline stood, queenly and magnanimous above us all. It was like waiting to be picked for the Hockey Team all over again. "Jean-Pierre" (with a fawning simper). "Claire" (with a wink). "Malcolm" (with a teasing kitten-smile). Our hearts churned. Sleeping rough on the streets of Moscow in this fierce cold with only a pair of Pyjama bottoms and a conspicuous pink-silk dress-suit for protection was not going to be pleasant. "You - You - what's your name?". "Laura" - gasped my friend with a gush of gratitude. "You and your friend - Kerry, isn't it? - you can come along too." Despite getting my name not even vaguely right, I could have kissed her. Almost crying with relief we bundled forward towards the van. "I'm not going without Russ" asserted Malcolm, heroically, though he didn't sound quite sure he meant it. "Russ?" pondered Caroline absently......"Oh, your little friend". Impotent now in his ailing flip-flops Russ buried his hand in his pocket and start plucking his leg hairs one by one. At least that's what we assumed he was doing from the little spasms of pain that ran across his face. "Oh, he can come too. We can fit just one more in can't we....can't we Boris?" she pleaded, simpering horribly in the moonlight. Boris concurred with a rough grunt and we all clambered into the truck.

It was slow progress in a 1970's Lada, through those parts of the city that no tourist guide would ever show you. Endless grey concrete facades peppered by windows that gaped like little mouths gulping for air in the stifling, smoky night air. Many of the buildings were derelict, the concrete run through with cracks, windows smashed, buildings half-demolished. Rusted trucks were abandoned in the central reservation. Boris turned all the lights off in the van. "If they see us all in here, we might get hijacked" explained Caroline. Her uppy-downy Minnie Mouse voice made us feel that that would be a good thing. "Apparently the station is the worst place, they wait for foreigners to come in from Siberia and mug them right there on the platform. The policemen know, but they get paid off, a pair of trainers or a few US dollars...". We shivered and all snuggled closer together. A car raced past us, its wheels screaming as it lurched from side to side, veering across the road. We carved sharply to the right to avoid being sliced across the front of the hood. From the car window we caught a flash of brilliant light and the crack of gunfire bursting into the night. "Down" shouted Boris, and we hunkered down for dear life until the squeal of wheels shrunk to a faint and distant hum. We drove past another abandoned car and a smoking shop window. The tinny squeal of an alarm wavered futilely in the darkness. And in the middle of it all an old lady walked her poodle as if the world was a good place that night.

About this time we started to wonder where we were actually headed. Perhaps we were to be sold into bondage as love slaves to rich Russian Potato-Kings. Perhaps our vital documentation would be confiscated and we'd spend our next few years hawking black-market tickets to Western Shows and importing Levi jeans. Perhaps we were to take part in a prominent government study examining the effects of an exclusive potato diet on the body and spirit of specially chosen subjects. Just then, we pulled up outside a block of flats that seemed to stretch endlessly above us into the darkness. Boris gathered all our luggage under one of his arms and dragged us into an elevator that reeked of urine and tobacco. We seemed to go up for an interminable length of time, finally reaching the twelfth floor after what seemed like minutes. Boris held the lift door open and led us all into a flat just opposite, number 912. It was a sudden taste of home that bought a lump to each of our throats. Armchairs lovingly draped in crocheted shawls, hand-hewn rugs, photos covering the walls, wall-paper the colour of marigolds, coffee tables and a radiogram and a stack of cuddly toys lined up along the sofa. Warmth too, and the smell of oranges, and the gurgle of running water clattering through pipes. We flung down our bags and paced, each one of us, around the room, enjoying the satisfying twang as our hamstrings reached full stretch for the first time in a week. Russ apparently sustained a groin injury from that first unaccustomed bout of exertion that haunts him even now.

Boris and Caroline then said their goodbyes and with a thinly veiled show of keeping their hands off each other departed into the black black night, leaving a stocky man called Yogi to keep an eye of us. Being the shortest, I won a space on a small two seater sofa, which others, though desirous, were overqualified for in the length department. Laura took a couple of cushions from my sofa, which was fine as we were friends, and everyone else improvised in one way or another to make a comfy bed.

JUST DUCK
WHEN YOU WALK PAST THE WINDOWS

I awoke many times during the night because Yogi insisted on looking out of the window every thirty seconds to check his car was still there, thereby bathing me at regular intervals with a blast of yellow light from the street outside. By about seven o'clock I thought I might as well take advantage of being awake and go and have a bath. There was real running water, hot at that, and soap, shampoo, conditioner. Suddenly, I wondered, as I sat naked in someone's bathtub liberally soaping myself with their soap, where exactly we were. Not one of us had thought to ask.

Fortunately Boris was able to resolve the issue. He returned just after nine o'clock with big black hollows under his eyes. (Russ's fevered imagination tormented him all the more now). It was, and this remained the official story, Boris' grandmother's flat. Given that the photos on the mantelpiece and bookshelf featured every kind of short black-haired son and grandson but none who looked like Boris, we were inclined to be doubtful but reluctant to look a gift horse in the mouth.

Still, Boris was going to find us somewhere to stay in the city that would release us from the bullying pedanticism of the Tourist Affairs Ministry and expose us to real Russian family life. We were unsure quite how real we wanted to go and felt that a few over-romanticised frills might not be altogether unwarranted, given our various brushes with the Russian underworld the previous night.

At midday he phoned to say he had somewhere for us to stay for the next four days, appearing shortly afterwards to take us there. We were the last to leave. Malcolm and Russ were already tucked up somewhere near the University. As we headed down in the elevator there was a man, apparently drunk but possibly dead, slumped in the corner of the elevator in a pile of pee an vomit. Boris gave him a sturdy kick. "There is much crime here", he told us, "Drugs, prostitution, fire-arms, immigration. Everyday we see someone dead somewhere. There are big men who control the streets, we have to tell them everything we do. They catch up with us if they want." He shrugged.

"Is there much work here?" we asked, noticing the large numbers of offices and shops that were boarded up and the dissolute looking people we saw trawling the streets and bins for litter and food. "There are some jobs, but the wages are so low, people are always trying to leave. Teachers, doctors, lawyers, they are paid nothing here, maybe three, four hundred roubles a week. To get a car costs ten thousand roubles, maybe thirty thousand on the black market. And then you cannot get the parts. It is impossible. You cannot live on Russian wages so people try and get out. There is not much food either. We know of people nearly starving to death because they can't afford food or can't stand in line".

"Where is your Grandmother now?"

"Oh, she's on holiday" said Boris, distractedly, suddenly intent on finding a piece of chewing gum that had fallen off the dashboard. A grim shiver ran up our spines.

YOU CAN NEVER MAKE ENOUGH JAM

We pulled up outside a tall grey block of flats. "Here we are. This is my friend Sergei's home. His mother is very friendly, she will look after you very well. You tell her what you need, she will help you." He led us up five flights of metal stairs and out onto a precarious looking metal balcony like a fire-escape that ran across to a cheery yellow door. A flustered looking lady with a warm, if anxious smile, and a stack of springy potato-coloured curls, answered the doors. She was fearsomely strong despite her size and carried both our rucksacks into the hallway in one incredible bound.

There was a room made up for us already, with a bed borrowed apparently from neighbours and an air mattress that was nicely padded out with comforters and pillows. The walls were decorated with posters of motorcycles and Kandisky's greatest works, an erroneous combination. On the dresser was a little jug of fresh flowers and a pitcher of cold drinking water next to two flowered cups. A curious spiky green plant and a row of home-made jams and unidentifiable pickled vegetables wobbled on the windowledge. It was rather dark in the room because the windows were blacked out so any window-cleaning immigration officials would not see us. We thanked her profusely, resorting to bows as a last resort (eighteen months of intense cultural programming in Japan had left us slightly unhinged) when communication irrevocably broke down.

Boris, thankfully, resolved our tactical and logistical difficulties in asking about payment. We were to pay Mrs Ivanovich five US dollars a night for the room with all foods supplied. It sounded criminally low but when we tried to pay more she insisted that was more than adequate. **The only stipulation, she outlined conspicuously, was that we actively "skulk" when in the apartment, especially when passing windows or** stretching to reach something from a high shelf. (Evidently right there on our arms we carried the taint of our alien status). Kneeling, she emphasised, was a very functional position, as well as sitting on short-legged stools or small wooden crates. Entering and leaving the apartment were also potentially loose links in the conspiracy so we must be careful to avoid arousing the suspicion of neighbours with vague or sinister behaviours. It was highly illegal to put up foreigners in this way, said Boris, but with three million visitors to Moscow a year and only seventy-two thousand hotel beds, it was a burgeoning, but nevertheless risky, expression of the entrepreneurial spirit of the average Muscovite. We nodded gravely and promised to be utterly utterly discreet.

A TRIP TO RED SQUARE

The next morning Mrs Ivanovich busied around making pasta and potatoes which were a generous and thoughtful if rather heavy compliment to the sausages and bread that already graced our plates. People here seemed excessively concerned about the dangers of a low-starch diet. We were incredibly touched knowing the relative scarcity and expense of items like sausages and knew that they had gone to special trouble. We filled out visibly in those few days and a greasy potato pallor came to hide the annoying exotic tan we'd been carrying around. By the time we got back to London we'd look like we'd never been away.

We asked Mrs Ivanovich what we should do with our day. She amiably suggested visiting a steam room where we could sweat our pores and enjoy being solidly beaten by a large Russian man armed only with a small towel and a small desiccated switch of oak twigs. Perhaps....... we said vaguely, holding out for a better offer. Later we would cunningly invent a mysterious skin condition that she'd offer to cure with a paste made from potatoes and aloe, that strangely green plant growing on our bedroom windowsill. In the meantime we asked - If the baths were closed, we faltered, where else would be good? No trip to Moscow, she told us, could be complete without a trip to Red Square. Inextricably intertwined with pivotal moments in Russia's history, it also betrayed Moscow's village origins, having started life as a small-town marketplace in the fourteenth century. While St Petersburg was always considered some kind of Prodigal son, with its frills and fancies and tobacco-smoking elegance, Moscow was its country-bumpkin mother with a straw in her mouth and dung on her heels.

As we walked through the backstreets to Red Square a hundred vignettes of timeless village life did seem to unfold from the chaos of the city streets. *Babushkas*, elderly women with frantically clicking knitting needles seemed lost in thought while their runny-nosed grandchildren skittered through back alleyways, their bare feet slapping on the greasy cobbles. Elderly men in secluded backstreets stamped wooden dominoes down on the table with a triumphant grunt or a ponderous hhrrmph and a swig of vodka. (In terms of average age of its permanent residents, Moscow is the oldest capital city in the world). Stressed looking younger women with babies strapped to their chests sold tomatoes from huge plastic crates in the middle of city thoroughfares. And in the distance we could always hear the music of violins played by serious looking young men with goatee beards Moscow's many subways.

There was a fairly cosmopolitan panache to Moscow's streets with slinky eyed thin-moustached men from middle-Asia mingling with the blue-eyed potato-coloured Russians. Most of the people we saw, except for the obviously care-free foreigners with their usual lolloping look of utter foolishness, wore a tense, resolute grimace as they battled through the crowded streets, especially the women, who seemed to do most of the running around in Russia, shepherding children to kindergartens and schools they could ill-afford, making frantic runs to the bakery or grocery store in their lunch hour, hauling bags of potatoes onto their shoulder for the long walk home.

We saw the spires of St Basil's cathedral long before we saw Red Square, dwarfed by the magnificent buildings of the Kremlin all along its one wall. The Cathedral was magnificent, a great tropical fruit salad of a building with its pineapple spikiness and the appley roundness of its nine towers. Inside the walls were decorated with patterns featuring Russian folk motifs, largely unintelligible to us but remarkable for their richness of colour and intricate designs and apparent focus on goats. We played hide and seek in the many tiny room inside the church until a stern looking woman with an impressive bonnet told us to stop.

There has been a Kremlin in Red Square for more than seven hundred years, built first of light wood, then sturdy oak, then white stone then finally the red stone that gave the marketplace its latest name. Its history is synonymous with the history itself. Russia's first famous madman connected with the Kremlin appears to have been Ivan the Terrible, whose name is justifiably associated with an astonishing record of cruelty and barbarism. (Given his penchant for pickled cabbage water and fermented meat dumplings, the name could have other connotations too). Bloodthirsty persecutor of Russian Christians, murderer of his own son, inscrutable womaniser, artless philosopher and appalling poet, his record is distinguished for all the wrong reasons. A fearsome proponent of the Russian Orthodox way, he collected wives like empty vodka bottles, invariably hastening their eventual demise through one devious device or another.

His bloody reign was followed by that of the Czars, a trumpeting bunch of dashing young men with an obsession about hair (they wore only fur undergarments and imposed a beard tax on hairy men) and a disproportionate number of offspring called Peter. They built lots of impressive looking buildings, tried to keep the Catholics out of Russia, drank lots and fornicated wildly. Napoleon, attracted to all the general debauchery, tried to take Moscow in 1812 and failed, but not before stealing all its potatoes and destroying many of Moscow's great buildings. An opportunistic mini industrial revolution saw Moscow's fortunes rebuilt with an emerging class of get-rich-quick merchants with guttural names rising from the ashes to challenge the foppish aristocracy. Then came lots of Czars called Alexander who tried to crush the peasants, an unpleasant bit of imagery given the size of some of these Czars with their endless potato feasts. This spawned a new Revolutionary Force led by some very angry men with gumboots and cattle prods and many secret societies led by geekish intellectuals with dodgy handshakes. Through their hard work, lots of good men were exiled to Siberia and serfdom was abolished, not before time. The country entered a new Capitalist era where people seemed to do nothing but drink tea and write endless poetry.

Now, of course, the different periods in the Kremlin's history have merged together and its hard to discern where history divides the citadel. We spent hours wandering around. Any visitor must leave the Kremlin punch drunk and wrestling in his mind with the contrast between the incredible riches they've seen and the relative poverty of the rest of the Russian people. Our heads reeled with images - beautiful cathedrals, mysterious towers, magnificent paintings, over-sized bells, egg-sized jewels, sculptures of the purest gold, endless endless icons and incredibly phallic cannons. It was magnificent, more so than any collection of monuments I have seen before or since, but their was a sourness when one thought about the people queuing for potatoes just a hundred yards beyond its walls.

At the other end of Red Square was Lenin's mausoleum, apparently constructed according to the squarest and most utilitarian of Soviet design principles. Lenin of course had overseen the formation of The Soviet Republic of Russia. He was a little man with strangely thin lips and a neat goatee beard that would finally be recognised as a major fashion force eighty years later when copied by a succession of disappointing British pop bands. He looked really quite relaxed in his plush little coffin, a little tense around the mouth but that was only to be expected. The polka dot tie was a jaunty, even foppish touch, a nice little testament to Lenin's ongoing belief in the value of careful accessorisation. The mausoleum was deathly silent, except a rather jolly wedding party who were leaning over the coffin to get the ultimate "Lenin at my wedding" photo-shot. One of the men carried a small bottle of vodka in his hand and a couple of glasses. They tried to angle the photograph so that Lenin appeared to be drinking from a small floral glass but inevitably tragedy ensued. It took a burly security guard to bring things to their logical conclusion and oust the revellers. People were crying as they filed past the coffin and a small lady with a big toilet roll doled out bundles of tissue to particularly distraught visitors.

In the years after the Revolution, Stalin had increasingly came to dominate Lenin's aides. When he eventually bullied his way to power by systematically eliminating any opposition, he equally systematically eradicated any self-consciousness, freedom of thought of sense of dignity of the Soviet People. Apparently he was entombed next to Lenin for eight years after his death in 1953 but apparently the embalmers had had rather an off day and small children were running screaming from the tomb, so they took him away and buried him under the Kremlin wall that he might fertilise small fruit trees.

WE TRIED TO BE ORTHODOX

Laura has an incredible voice which thankfully she invests in beautiful classical pieces (notorious for her penchant for men in tights and fascination with unlikely mediaeval instruments) rather than tabletop recantations of famous show-tunes. Her knowledge of classical pieces and fascination with the tormented souls who wrote them is second to none. So when she realised that Prokofiev was buried within five miles of where we were staying, we had, of course, to visit his gravesite. No holiday, I always said, was complete without a trip to see a dead musician's grave. I was glad we had gone, though. There was a quiet ambience to the peaceful cemetery where two or three old men with empty vodka bottles chimed toasts to some of Moscow's favourite heroes. There was kindness as well as suffering here. Imbued with a touching new sense of the Muscovite spirit, we set off on the Metro to find a Russian Orthodox Church. No Muscovite we met could use the word " Metro" without a lump the size of a weasel welling in his throat, rightly so, for it is clean, efficient, inordinately cheap and beautifully ordained with Mosaic designs along the length of every platform. The whole effect was like some kind of dry bar on wheels, with the soft lighting and elegant trickle of elevator music. Everyone seemed to be reading, ploughing through this or that Dostoyevsky first edition, translated Danielle Steel novel or latest work by Gabrielle Garcia Marquez. For the first time on our trip, no one gave us a second glance when we brought out our guidebooks.

Though not truly familiar with the Russian Orthodox faith, we hoped to imbibe a little of the spirit of Mother Russia though immersion in a religious service steeped in history and the soul of the Russian people. We were early, and stood around feeling uncomfortably disrespectful in our tatty shoes and fraying skirts. I struggled awkwardly with the stiff mesh of wire-like frizz that my hair turned into within a day of washing it. Everyone else who filed in seemed to have their hair covered with a chaste little scarf or shawl. I had yet to meet the piece of fabric that could keep my curls down.

The Church itself, inconspicuous from the outside, was magnificent inside, ornate and gold-rimmed with glorious turquoise and orange paintwork and an incredible domed ceiling. The music started not long after we arrived, deep and melodious, barely audible at times. The priest, a serious looking man in black robes with a long winding beard swung a large incense container around and a delicious perfumed haze started to fill the church. I stifled a sneeze as the unaccustomed fog of powdery sandalwood invaded my body cavities. Fortunately I reduced a potential sneeze outbreak to a mere attack of the hiccups. We tried to look inconspicuous as a soft murmuring filled the Church. Everyone seemed to know the words. Miming was hopeless, the diphthongs these people were using had no place yet in my repertoire of haunting yet strangely Flemish sounds. So we hummed our own tunes, me something by Billy Joel, Laura something rather more lofty, and felt some sense of communion with the other hummers around us.

The service was long, and we stood all the way through in the Russian way, enjoying the rush of music swishing over us, the powdery incense that dusted our clothes and the warm smell of oranges that was later localised to an old man in the back row. Not speaking Russian, most of the deeper philosophy went over our ignorant heads but it was magical and haunting and steeped in the kind of ritual that we had not seen since leaving Japan. As the wax dripped steadily from the innumerable candles, we caught a sense of the progression of Russia's history through the last five hundred years.

EXCUSE ME MISS, YOU FORGOT YOUR...

He was definitely following us. Conspicuous in an orange plastic Mac and a straw hat he galloped down the escalator. In a flurry of desperation we flung ourselves through the electric turnstile. While the European model is traditionally a benign device designed to deter fare-dodgers, and impart a mild tap to an errant hip, the The Russian "*hip-crusher*" model with its added *testicular scrunch* feature (Sergei mimed this to us late one night after a particularly heady game of Gin Rummy and a fierce Italian sausage supper) could ruin one's chances of ever having children. Just at the moment I plunged through the turnstile two large chunks of cast-iron swung out from either side to crush my hips in a grisly embrace that would have brought me screaming to my knees had I not pinned upright at the hips and therefore restricted to a limp flopping forward at the waist. I felt like a trout snared on a hook, and all the time the man in the orange Mac was gaining. Wrenching myself free with an anguished howl I lurched forward again. Laura made a break for it too and miraculously escaped only with the loss of a kagoul pocket and a few curls. We dreaded to think what damages the Russian Transport Service could inflict if you didn't have a ticket. If we died making a run for it through the barriers they'd find our tickets in our pockets and martyr us. For years after they'd talk about our senseless deaths. We hoped.

Just then, a train pulled into the station and we leapt on it, gasping and slightly shaken. But just at the moment the doors started to close the man in the orange Mac leapt like James Bond through the closing doors. We dashed through the train into the next compartment, leaving a flurry of small children and old people knocked down like skittles in our wake. Out of the corner of our eye a flash of orange (later localised to an old lady's shopping bag) terrorised us and we leapt screaming and wild-haired like banshees into the next carriage causing one young man to choke on what looked like a potato burrito. Just then the train started to slow down. We were approaching a station. We jigged on the spot like children desperately needing the toilet, keeping a wild and paranoid eye on the door from the next compartment. Pretty soon everyone else had started watching it too. A generalised hysteria seemed to be sweeping the carriage. The train screamed to a halt and we hunkered up ready to spring onto the platform with the kind of athletic bound favoured by the new generation of superhero action figures. The man in the orange Mac was sure to be watching the platform. We knew his game, and we weren't afraid to play it. If a waiting game was what he was after, that was what he would get. Timing was critical. We had to wait long enough for the orange man to think we weren't getting off, but not so long that the train pulled away before we could get off. We waited and waited and then finally, at what we judged was the last possible minute, we staged our athletic exit. Handicapped by rather less lycra and rather more hair than Spiderman ever had, we eventually achieved a limp tumble rather than a firm-buttocked spring but it got us off the train. But the fat lady hadn't sung and it wasn't over yet. The train driver, unbeknown to us, was enjoying a leisurely cup of coffee in the secluded privacy of his air-conditioned cabin. Out of the corner of our eye we made out a flash of orange. The man in the Mac had made a leap for the platform. We leapt back on and the orange man leapt back on....it was like some kind of frenetic step class for today's busy commuting lifestyle. We were getting quite dizzy. The people in our carriage watched in bemusement. Of course they couldn't see the man in the orange Mac, just our sweaty and pointless acrobatics. Just then the train's bells started ringing and we each tried to outguess the other. We were in, he was out. The bells rang again and someone started hollering. Public opinion inside the compartment was divided. Some people were pushing us, some urging us to stay. Someone grabbed hold of Laura and starting pulling her back in. They seemed worried we were going to jump one time too many. Perhaps this kind of maniacal leaping from trains was seen as a kind of Russian "playing chicken" or worse that than, a desperate cry for help. We leapt one last time, achieving some sort of athletic glory as our backpack straps snagged on the door and send us somersaulting across the platform. Just as we leapt out, the orange man leapt in - then with one final lurch, the doors slammed shut, finally and irrevocably. The man in the orange cape and strangely floppy hat was left to wave at us with an anguished expression from behind the train doors.

We were quick to bury ourselves in the crowd, in case the orange man had pulled the emergency whistle and stopped the train in the tunnel. So despite the conspicuous absence of a pursuer, which lent a certain mystery to our sweaty dash through the ticket office and out into Maxim Gorsky Avenue, we ran at speed for at least another ten minutes. When we finally stopped, a lurking paranoia continued to haunt us for quite a few hours. It was the logical conclusion to our ongoing vigilance for immigration officials. We'd been bottling it up for too long. We were quite enjoying this Cagney & Lacey style subterfuge. I had always wanted to be a Bond girl but lacked the fundamental credentials. Now, if anyone followed us for more than five consecutive footsteps, we'd make convoluted about-turns and cunning route deviations to foil our would-be pursuers. It took ages for us to get anywhere but we felt deliciously mysterious. We never did find out who the man in the orange Mac was but Laura later discovered she'd left a small pocket notebook on the bench next to Prokofiev's tomb. The thought that the man we'd put through hoops was in fact a good citizen trying to reunite Laura with her lost property was not a nice one. But, of course, cautioned Laura, the voice of reason, he could have been an Immigration Official secretly masquerading as a good citizen trying to reunite Laura with her lost property. When in doubt, we agreed, it was best to be suspicious.

CAN I INTEREST YOU IN A BUCKET?

Later that afternoon, when we finally relaxed our guard, a man of about thirty rushed up to me and said, with a great deal of gesturing - "you want bucket?".

Bucket?

"Bucket?"

Bucket?. He gestured for us to stay still while he ran off to fetch something, presumably the bucket he was trying to get rid of. Inwardly intrigued, yet outwardly disinterested, we made excuses to hang around for a few minutes. The man returned shortly afterwards bearing a huge bouquet of succulent gladioli blooms, five or six fat stems dripping pollen and a delicious summery ripeness from their dizzy blossoms. He gave us the flowers with a bow and told us we were beautiful. We couldn't close our minds to the possibility that this could be a scam engineered by immigration officials to expose our soft underbellies and bring us crawling on our hands and knees to Daddy Yeltsin so we viewed him cautiously out of the corner of one eye the way they do in films, which made us look somewhere between lascivious and palsied. This seemed to incite him further, driving him to exhortations of a greater and greater magnitude. It seemed be wanted to marry us, which was touching, if a little impractical. He seemed nice though, friendly with a beautiful warm smile. However, conversation soon dried up. There was little to talk about except the weather and the magnificent flowers. We did thank him profusely in as many languages as we could think of but eventually even this had to come to an end. We shared only three words - "beautiful", "MacDonalds" and "Bucket" (we think he meant bouquet) and we could only find so many intelligible permutations of the three. (We think we concurred on "George Harrison" but couldn't be sure it was the same George Harrison). So we left after a while, clutching our bunch of gladioli, to find MacDonalds.

MacDonalds was crowded beyond our wildest expectations. The queues wound around the side of the building and around the edge of a kind of 1960's strip mall. We joined the end, salivating profusely despite our limply vegetarian leanings, (imposed more than necessity than choice over recent months), at the thought of a ground beef patty and a liberal helping of gherkins, which was strange, as I was renowned for my pathological aversion to decaying vegetables, however effectively preserved. Eventually our turn came, and we stuttered with excitement through almost every item on the menu. I ordered extra gherkins. The food was amazing. Unlike almost every other culinary experience we'd endured on this trip, it tasted exactly how we'd expected it to taste. While me munched, eyes half-closed in ecstasy (half-open to keep a watchful guard on our gladioli) a group of drunken men from Georgia menaced us with talk of drugs and knives and border raids. We politely declined their offer of hard-core opiates to sprinkle on our burgers. We were both aware that a bundle of limp gladioli would wield little serious authority in a skirmish with a knife-wielding Georgian guerrilla so we explained, firmly but politely we thought, that we didn't get involved in drugs and hoped to finish our burgers in peace. Sounding very much like London woosies and proud of it, we endured a crushing round of unintelligible but certainly scathing comments about girls. (Generally we tried to avoid talking in public in case plain-clothes immigration officials were out stalking the streets so we avoided any retaliation). But the food was so good, we didn't care. We had seconds, and thirds if I remember rightly, and only vacated our seats when a feeling of utter nausea and the sensation of pure liquid fat oozing through our pores set in. Then we ran as fast as we could through the streets in case the Georgians were lying in wait for us.

That night we went out in search of food that didn't feature potato as its main ingredient. Having never actually reached the Gum Department Store earlier that day, we decided that was as likely a place as any to find a restaurant. The area of Red Square just outside the store, which runs along one whole side was lined with Artists offering portraits of cute children, winsome pets, troublesome in-laws or prominent Moscow landmarks. I wasn't what sure which category we fell into but we received a few offers nevertheless.

The store itself, built at the turn of the century, personified the old wedding cake phenomenon at its pastel-coloured height. It was an amazing pale blue creation, three long hallways under a domed glass roof. Judging by the seething crowds that bustled and jostled to get in, we expected to find ourselves enmeshed in a sticky shopping extravaganza with all kinds of shops and boutiques (as the Intourist Guide Book promised) so overflowing with luxury goods that lucky customers could take their pick. Disappointingly we found only a small shop selling bubble bath and some kind of music store that was out of albums and singles and thought they'd heard of compact discs but weren't quite sure..... Not even a single solitary potato.

Fortunately we got home to find Mrs Ivanovich making yet more jam and cooking potatoes to go with our sausages. I wondered how often she had to shop to feed what she seemed to imagine were our gargantuan Western appetites. Each night we sat down to at least seven sausages each. We tried to tell her we didn't need to eat so much but we never successfully made our point. We dreaded to think what it must be costing her. She smiled at us in a tired sort of way as we came through the door. A young man reclined on the sofa in the Russian equivalent of a vest with some superhero goddess astride a motorbike emblazoned on his chest. Despite that my heart let out a small skip and I felt a simpering bashfulness steal all over me. "My son, Sergei", she volunteered from the kitchen. I smiled and knew immediately I looked ridiculous, all gums and no teeth.

He looked us up and down then turned back to his magazine, all the while chewing on a cigarette but. His mum came in and switched on the television. Vremya, a topical news and current affairs program, was showing. Unlike most fairly self-congratulatory Russian broadcasts, this one tended to adopt a less eulogising view of Russian life, and in balance a less deprecating one of the rest of the world. Tonight the showed Japanese game show contestants stuffing live eels down their pants in pursuit of stardom. They couldn't have made the rest of the world look any bleaker.

BUT HE'S ... DEAD, ISN'T HE?

The next morning Laura and I separated for a few hours. I headed along Arbat Street, billed by the guide-book as a kind of Russian Carnaby Street, with street vendors and craft stalls flanking every inch of the sidewalk. I was desperately thirsty (it must have been nearly thirty degrees) and I was looking for a sign that suggested a pleasing liquid refreshment with a low-potato content. An ambiguous sign that seemed to be written in blood on some kind of chalkboard led me through an opening in a back alley. In front of me two doors beckoned, one of which presumably led to the bar. I chose the right hand door, feeling suddenly like one of those characters in a computer game, and groped my way up a flight of stairs in virtual darkness.

I felt my way through a heavy padded door, expecting to find light and the reassuring clink of ice in glasses. Instead I found myself standing in complete darkness. I could make nothing out except the rattle of my own breathing, a faint tang of patchouli and the muted crooning of some kind of Russian George Michael tinkling from hidden speakers. Then, suddenly, I became aware of a dim light in the corner of the room. Then another, in the opposite corner, and a third right ahead of me. Peering through the murky halflight I thought I saw a man standing there, looking right at me, his arm outstretched in some kind of sweeping oratorical gesture. It seemed to be coming straight for my throat. I leapt straight up in the air and let out a whoop of horror like those strangely squeaky young men always did in The Nancy Drew mysteries. Then in the other corner of the room, the stiff-suited outline of a weasely man in shiny shoes peeled itself away from the darkness. If I wasn't very much mistaken, and here I had to ask myself some pretty probing questions about the contents of my last coffee, it was Lenin, in a disappointingly shabby little three-piece suit with a particularly savage parting ripping right across the top of his head. Outside in the street the menacing cackle of a grown man in tights performing distasteful disappearing acts with live ferrets paled into a sanitary blandness next to the exhumation of former Russian Presidents that unfolded before me. There was Gorbachov, looking startled to see Lenin, and Kruschev, fat and boorish and rambunctious-looking in a shiny suit. Neither of them looked good. There was a hepatic pallor to their yellowing cheeks and strangely black teeth. Then Brezhnev, Stalin ...... out they all popped from the darkness in eerie slow-motion like recalcitrant guests at a surprise birthday party. So surreal was the gradual unfolding of dead premiers that I had failed to notice the roar of blood and raw animal fear that charged through my ears. I wondered if The Christian Scientists had got to me at last. Just then I heard a rustle behind me and the creaking open of a heavy vinyl-padded door. I feared that one of the strangely angular Russian leaders was making a quick getaway. I remembered my morbid childhood preoccupation with the mad old lady in Mr Rochester's attic (Jane Eyre was a very sinister story) and wondered if Russian presidents didn't die, they just went mad and underwent a cryogenically-facilitated suspension of vital functions in a small black room above a Russian bar. I was sure I had seen something about it on the X-files so it must be true. Just them someone sneaked up behind me and coughed. I screamed like a wild woman just at the moment the lights flickered on. A dapper little man with a handkerchief in his top pocket smiled back at me. "You like our celebrities?"

"Aren't they - ?"

"Dead, yes. But the miraculous process of paraffinic regeneration supported by a whole new breed of software dedicated to recreating high-profile personalities has opened new doors in the synthetic celebrity life-form business"

"You mean they're wax?".

"Why yes. You didn't think they were real did you?"

"Nah, course not", I rebuffed, cuffing him in a winsome and playful way with my fist as we joked about what a ninny that would make me. It wasn't the sort of uninvited physical combat I would normally enter into with a Russian Christian Scientist (not on our first meeting anyway) but the moment seemed strangely right. Unfortunately I misfired in the half-darkness and deposited a sturdy ringer on the left side of his nose. He took it very well.

The waxworks had been opened just that month after many years of careful research into the exact distribution pattern of Lenin's birthmarks and a close study of Kruschev's hair-line. The unlikely premise was that people who had missed the chance to see these Great Leaders while they were alive could somehow fool themselves that Lenin/Kruschev/Breshnev** (delete as applicable depending on fantasy - the deluxe Lenin fantasy package featured three red-headed Russian soldiers and a free potato breakfast) - had returned to life for the express purpose of making the acquaintance of say a Boris, or a Dmitri, or a Natalia from 1990's downtown Moscow. It was proving popular with older housewives, commented the man with the polka dot handkerchief and - here he leant towards me in a conspiratorial way and put a brotherly hand on my shoulder (evidently that cuff had been a little too friendly, despite the bloodshed that ensued) - "not all of them widows". I tried not to think too much about that as I headed out to the street to find that the disappearing ferret act had come a little unhinged. (The ferrets had apparently staged a mutiny. One of them was presently attached to the finger of a small child who had prodded it one time too many with an ice-lolly stick.) If this was Carnaby Street I hoped I never had to see Soho.

ANYONE CARE FOR OPERA?

We had decided, fresh from our infusion of Carnaby Street culture, to try and see an opera before we went home to England. "Tchaikovsky's Greatest Hits" was billed at one of Moscow's older theatres and tickets were still available so we decided to spend our last night at an orgy of musical ecstasy. All would have gone well had Laura and myself not managed to lose each other sometime during the day. Half an hour before the opera, we had still not found each other. I was running like a headless chicken through Moscow's underground system, having neither the tickets, the map, nor the address of the theatre, plaguing big Russians with nonsensical questions which roughly translated as "Where does Tchaikovsky live these days?". Naturally I received little in the way of serious replies although one old lady seemed to tell me he was alive and well and living in a small broom closet in her basement suite.

Eventually I dropped my face into my hands to ponder my fate. Then I heard, in the slickest Queen's English, a young man's voice say

"Can we help you?". He was an angel sent apparently from Kazakhstan, where his family grew wine, to save my life. I outlined my difficulties and he and his mother set off with small notebooks to take detailed statements and route maps from each of the passengers on board the train. Their smart clothes seemed to command an ominous authority. Having compiled a detailed itinerary, they steered me off onto another subway line and insisted on accompanying me all the way to the theatre. For people without credit cards, the queues to buy tickets for productions at the bigger theatres were colossal, hours and hours of waiting. People think, said the young man, that Russians only queue for Levi jeans or American leather jackets. He, apparently, once spent a whole night waiting in line to purchase a subscription to the Complete Works of William Shakespeare.

The young man's name was Frederic and he was holidaying with his mother Martha in the home of a rich uncle who lived on the right side of town. His overwhelming ambition in life was to become a Doctor and he was trying to drum up some sponsorship from family and friends while he was staying in the city. He was bright enough, his mother said, to be a doctor, but you needed money to buy your way into one of the few medical schools open to boys from Kazakhstan. He was still in secondary school now, but working hard and entering all the Western essay competitions he could to win money and buy his place in medical school. So far he'd won a year's supply of cornflakes and a small matchbox car, all of which were lying in a Kazakhtan postal depot awaiting payment of the massive postal tarrifs. At weekends he worked as a porter in a mortuary. It was the closest, he said, he could get to patients. His mother was obviously very proud of him and they seemed to be very close. When we finally reached the theatre, (all of us running because the performance had started thirty minutes ago) I gurgled them a heartfelt thankyou between gulps of air and we exchanged addresses. I never did find out where they had been going when I'd interrupted their plans almost two hours earlier.

The performance had started already. Fortunately Laura had left my ticket at the Box Office for me to collect but I wasn't allowed in until the interval, (although I was allowed to listen from behind a fire door, which reduced the performance to a muffled panting interrupted only by an occasional farting sound. I wasn't sure that was the effect Tchaikovsky had been striving for). As our tickets were for the highest seats in the gods, I doubted the usher's theory that my near-invisible entrance would completely unhinge these highly strung musicians, but having no experience in operatic melodramatics, I was in no position to argue. When eventually I was allowed in I was surprised to find an overly tall man in a baseball cap sitting in Laura's place. Laura must be here since my ticket was here, I reasoned with only the slightest murmur of panic. I waited patiently for climactic flashes of light to reveal a motley scattering of fat, shiny and thinning crowns glinting beneath me like pearls in the bottom of the ocean. Despite the lack of serious contenders, it was several minutes before I located Laura's tumbling curls. She would have been almost within reach if I'd had my twenty-seven metre arm extension to hand. Instead I calculated an optimum trajectory for my polo mint and launched the missile, vertical of course to cleverly minimise air-resistance, from the edge of the railing with a carefully delivered flick of my finger. It hurtled skyward with a ballistic whirr before falling, slowly, slowly, slowly...to land on the head of a fat man in red trousers. Here was someone not wearing brown. Evidently this was a very special night. Given this propensity for scarlet legwear (I hadn't yet seen his canary yellow body-stocking), further accessorisation with a polo-mint hair adornment seemed a minor matter.

The commotion and strange stinging sensation that ensued (remember that a penny falling from the top of the Eiffel tower can kill you) awoke most of that round gentleman's row. Laura, sitting just three metres away, was roused from reverie but remained pleasantly confused. I waved at her frantically from my godly platform (to the annoyance of the tall man in the baseball cap), but she still didn't see me. Only when the next interval came was I able to make a frantic dash to intercept her just as she headed to the lady's washroom. Happily reunited and co-joined now in adjacent seats (the usher had offered her an upgrade to a better seat for the cost of an ice-cream) we settled down to watch the rest of the performance. It was a fittingly chaotic, yet ultimately serene end to our trip.

SORRY, DIDN'T YOU WANT ME TO SHUT THE DOOR?

The next morning we awoke in a flutter of nervous desperation, a rage of utter excitement and a damp trickle of disappointment. It was the last morning we would spend on foreign soil for a while. By six o'clock Russian time we would be back in England drinking coffee at inflated airport prices while we waited for our fathers' friendly beards to pop up over the Arrivals barrier. It was a sobering thought.

Sergei had deliberately chosen to breakfast that morning in a transparent vest top which unhinged me further. Mindful that this was my last opportunity to win his favours I tried to infuse "do you want sausage?" with as much sexual allure as possible while retaining my veneer of virginly virtuosity. He seemed untouched by the challenge, stabbing manfully at the ground meat product in a way that made his biceps ripple. I was almost crooning but Laura kicked me under the table and I took a good hold on myself.

Mrs Ivanovich busied around making some early-morning jam and cooking our potato breakfast while we packed. I made a conspicuous and unnecessary point of identifying England on Sergei's world-map. I added my address just next to the Isle of Man, making it look like a casual afterthought, and mentioned wistfully how all my life I'd been looking for a Russian penpal. Laura kicked me again.

Sergei headed out to work at around nine o'clock, blissfully unmindful of the emotional upheaval he'd stirred in my bosom, and I stifled a whimper. But there was quite a lot to do and Laura was getting quite bossy (she later told me it was for my own good). Suddenly aware of the time, (it had taken an hour or so to get through breakfast) we gathered all our bags together and started to move towards the door just as Mrs Ivanovich began cooking some kind of egg dish. It was hard to tear her away from the kitchen once she got going. I hoped she shopped often and bought little.

We called to her from the hallway, not wanting to trek our hiking boots through the front room. She looked a little surprised that we were going but helped us carry all our bags onto the landing outside the flat, all of us crouching low to avoid exposing ourselves to the neighbours. Laura pulled the door behind us to keep the heat in. We all stopped dead. A car beeped in the street below and a man in a fur hat bellowed up to us in impatient manly tones. I had half-hoped it was Sergei coming home to pick me up and whirl me away for a lifetime of mutually unintelligible happiness like the closing scene in An Officer and a Gentleman. But it was our taxi driver. And Mrs Ivanovich stood stranded on her balcony in the cold with an egg dish bubbling on the stove behind a locked door. We were mortified. So was Mrs Ivanovich. Her whole face started to slide down into a wretched expression that just about had us in tears. It was an appalling situation. I have to say, she was incredibly brave and stoic in the face of such a disaster, heroic in fact, waving us on our way while her flat smouldered under clouds of eggy smoke. We tried to stay and help her break in but she was quite insistent that we catch our plane. In retrospect she probably wanted us out of the way before we could do any more damage.

We were not catching the taxi all the way to the airport, just to the Intourist Hotel. (That place we should have been staying in for the past few days). It was a fairly imposing building in a glass and concrete kind of way, with a large front lobby where Mars bars and luxury western sanitary equipment could be purchased for the right nod and wink. (The wrong one could put you in touch with a burly man named Peter who would slap you all over with a small birch tree for a nominal charge.)We hung about the hotel lobby for a while, trying to emulate the haughty smoothness adopted by a party of strangely loose-hipped Frankfurtans as they sipped curiously green cappuccinos and held some kind of public demonstration against chain-store underwear. There was lots of mutually encouraged poking and prodding which, perhaps, inevitably, culminated in tragedy when a shiny-headed man called Frederick dropped his biscotti down the front of Helmut's Calvin Kleins. We felt his pain. Fortunately at that point the bell rang and after a little skirmish involving what appeared to be some nipple-tweaking, the Frankfurtans got up to leave. We attached ourselves to the back of their party and dribbled behind them right onto the Intourist Airport Shuffle, which was of course technically reserved for patrons of the Intourist Hotel. But the driver didn't bat an eye and before we could shout "hold on to your knickers" we were pulling away into the early Moscow morning, airport, and home, bound.

It was the end of a trip that had taken us about 12,000 miles, almost all on land, and exposed us to experiences I don't think we could even have dreamt of. (Note that this is not invariably a good thing!). We had learnt that without risk, opportunities are limited. To not make a trip until you're totally prepared is like waiting for all the traffic lights to turn green. We probably confused, even offended whole nations with our fumbling soliloquies patched from our small library of phrase books, our endless, pedantic obsession with the exact contents of our meals, our strange dairy odour and our unsanitary nose-blowing and snot-retainment habits. But in our defence, we really did try to learn as much as we could about the countries we visited, both before, during and after, which is, I feel, every traveller's obligation.

Though life has remained fairly exciting since our trip, and Laura and I have both travelled to far and distant places, I have never again felt the intoxicating blend of fear, recklessness, sensory overstimulation and utter, utter excitement that fuelled this, our first big adventure. It is curious now, looking back, to see how the experiences I enjoyed then set the course for many of the choices I would later make: perhaps because you learn when travelling that the strangest sounding ideas can make perfect sense if you just give them a try...

HAPPY TRAVELLING!

ACKNOWLEDGMENTS

To Nick, for everything!

To Laura, for being such a wonderful and inspiring travel companion and for trusting me to tell our ales....

To my family for letting me loose on the world and trusting me to come back!